What a Character!

FAMOUS AMERICAN STATESMEN

Notable Lives from History

Marilyn Boyer

First printing: September 2024

Copyright © 2024 by Marilyn Boyer and Master Books. All rights reserved. No part of this book may be reproduced, copied, broadcast, stored, or shared in any form whatsoever without written permission from the publisher, except in the case of brief quotations in articles and reviews. For information write:

Master Books, P.O. Box 726, Green Forest, AR 72638

Master Books® is a division of the New Leaf Publishing Group, LLC.

ISBN: 978-1-68344-368-1
ISBN: 978-1-61458-883-2 (digital)
Library of Congress Control Number: 2024943361

Cover: Diana Bogardus
Interior: Terry White

Please consider requesting that a copy of this volume be purchased by your local library system.

Printed in the United States of America

Please visit our website for other great titles:
www.masterbooks.com

For information regarding promotional opportunities, please contact the publicity department at pr@nlpg.com.

Table of Contents

1. Benjamin Franklin—Statesman, Inventor, and Patriot 5
2. Samuel Adams—Son of Liberty 17
3. Patrick Henry—The Voice of the Revolution 29
4. John Hancock—Dedicated Patriot 43
5. Alexander Hamilton—Designer of American Government 57
6. Henry Clay—The Great Peacemaker 71
7. Francis Scott Key—The Star-Spangled Banner 83
8. Daniel Webster—Defender of the Constitution 97
9. Sam Houston—Hero of Texas 109
10. William Jennings Bryan—Champion of the Common Man ... 123

Glossary 139

Corresponding Curriculum 147

Endnotes 149

Image Credits

Images are AI-generated at shutterstock.com

Benjamin Franklin – Statesman, Inventor, and Patriot

January 17, 1706 – April 17, 1790

Who Was Benjamin Franklin?

Benjamin Franklin was one of the most significant men in early America. He was well known throughout the world for his wisdom and many achievements. A printer by trade, Ben Franklin was an author, an inventor, a statesman, and a scientist. He was instrumental in helping our country obtain its freedom. When the United States became an independent nation, Benjamin Franklin was there, making sure it started out and stayed on the right track.

Early Days

Benjamin Franklin was born on January 17, 1706, in Boston, Massachusetts. He had 16 brothers and sisters. His father was a soapmaker and candlemaker. As a boy, Ben was full of fun. His friends often followed his lead. One day, he and his friends found a pile of building stones close to the water's edge. Ben had an idea. He persuaded his friends to help him build a wharf from which they could go fishing. That evening, the boys hauled the stones down to the water.

They left for home, having put a fine-looking wharf in place. They could hardly wait to go fishing on it the next day. However, when workmen who were building a new house arrived in the morning, they were extremely upset to see their stones reformed into a fishing wharf. Immediately, they tried to find out who had done it. They discovered Ben Franklin was the leader. Ben defended his actions. He told his father it was a good wharf and the boys needed it. His father said, "The

stones were not yours to take, Ben, and what is not honest cannot be truly useful."[1] So Ben learned a lesson he would never forget — that "honesty is the best policy."[2] Of course, the boys had to make it right and carry all those heavy stones back to where they had found them.

Schooling

Ben went to the local grammar school when he was eight years old. He was at the top of the class in reading and writing. He did not attend school for long, unfortunately. When he was 10 years old, he had to leave school and go to work for his father. His father was a hard worker, but he didn't make much money and couldn't send Ben to college. No one could have guessed that one day Ben would be awarded degrees by various colleges and universities. He later said, "The door to learning is never closed."[3]

Ben did not enjoy candlemaking, though, and soon his father decided to **apprentice** him to his older brother James, who was already a succesful printer. Apprenticeship meant that Ben would have to work for James until he was 21 years old. It was hard work, and James was not easy to work for, but Ben applied himself to learn the job. He spent all of his spare time improving his mind. He often stayed up reading late into the night.

Ben made a deal with James concerning meals. James had been buying food for Ben, but Ben asked for the money instead, to buy food for himself. Since he ate simply, he could save half of what his brother gave him. With the money Ben saved, he bought books. Ben also made better use of time. He would eat a few raisins and bread, or rice and boiled potatoes while the other printers went to eat lunch at the boarding house. With his extra time, Ben, of course, would read.

apprentice: Make one learn a trade from a skilled worker

Writing

Ben began writing pieces for his brother's newspaper but signed them as Mrs. Silence Dogood. He did not want to let his brother know he was the real author of the articles. He would just slip them under the print shop door. People loved them, and

Famous American Statesmen

everyone wondered who Silence Dogood was. Ben eventually told James, but sadly, James grew jealous of the attention and praise Ben received. He treated Ben very harshly.

In the fall of 1723, Ben left James' print shop and headed for New York, 200 miles from home. He decided he would make his own way in the world. Ben could not find a job in New York, so he tried Philadelphia. He was tired and dirty from traveling when he got there. His coat pockets were stuffed with extra clothes. Upon arriving in town, he bought three large rolls from the baker. He walked down the street, eating one and carrying the other two under his arms. Young Deborah Read, who lived

in Philadelphia, was standing in the doorway of her father's home and saw him walking down the street. He was an amusing sight. She had no way of knowing he would one day be her husband. He finally got a job with a printer in Philadelphia. After several years and more hardships, he opened his own print shop there.

Ben's Many Accomplishments

Ben did marry Deborah Read. Together, they worked hard to make their print business succesful. Ben began writing an almanac called *Poor Richard's Almanack*. It contained loads of practical tips, weather

forecasts, word puzzles, and useful information. He gave tips on gardening, planting crops, and housekeeping. The *Almanack* included many of Ben's sayings which became famous, such as: "There are no gains without pains," "He who lies down with dogs wakes up with fleas," "Early to bed, early to rise, makes a man healthy, wealthy, and wise."[4] Ben and Deborah began to grow wealthy. They were very generous with their money. They gave to charities, including the famous **evangelist** George Whitefield, to help support his **orphanage**.

Benjamin Franklin did much to make Philadelphia a better place to live. He donated money for **cobblestones** to line the muddy streets. He also developed a street cleaning system, started the first Pennsylvania militia, published the first novel ever in America, and owned and published the leading newspaper of its time. Along with all this, he built the first electrical battery, organized the first fire department and the first postal system, helped start the first public library in the American colonies so people could check out books to read, and helped to build a hospital. Later, he even founded the University of Pennsylvania.

evangelist: Traveling preacher of the Gospel

orphanage: Home to raise children who have no parents

cobblestones: Small round stones placed along the edges of streets

10   Famous American Statesmen

Ben invented the famous Franklin stove to heat houses efficiently, as well as the first lightning rod to keep houses from burning down if struck by lightning, **bifocal** glasses so people could see better, and a glass harmonica and other musical instruments. Along with all these things, he also improved carriage wheels, windmills, water wheels, and so much more that it would fill many pages to tell. He never applied for patents for his inventions. Patents were permits securing for a term of years the right to exclude others from making, using, or selling an invention. This was because he wanted people to benefit from them; he did not make them to earn money for himself.

> **bifocal:** Lenses for both close and distant vision

Ben the Statesman

The people of Pennsylvania loved and trusted Ben Franklin. He was elected clerk of the Assembly of Pennsylvania and later, a lawmaker in that same assembly. For ten years, he was re-elected to help make laws for the colony. At this time, it was just a colony, not a state. In 1754, he was sent to make a treaty with the

Benjamin Franklin — Statesman, Inventor, and Patriot   11

Iroquois people. He had accomplished all this while Patrick Henry was still a boy and George Washington was still a surveyor.

When conflict started with England, Benjamin Franklin, with his years of wisdom, was a perfect choice to send there. His mission was to try to **negotiate** peace with Great Britain. Ben tried to explain to the British government how the colonists felt about the various taxes being forced upon them. At first, most of the colonists wanted to remain under the leadership of King George III. Ben was sent to **appeal** to the king and **Parliament**. He wrote articles explaining how the taxes were harmful to the colonists. He spoke before Parliament on behalf of the colonies. He was finally able to get them to **repeal** the Stamp Act. His job wasn't done yet, though. He remained in England for eight more years trying to get fair treatment for the colonists. It was a long, long time to be away from his family! He spent hours talking with the great English statesman William Pitt, who spoke up in Parliament on behalf of the colonists. Pitt introduced a bill in Parliament trying to get Parliament to treat the colonists with respect, but it did not pass. It looked like all attempts at avoiding a war would fail.

negotiate: Reach an agreement on

appeal: Make a serious request

Parliament: The ruling body of England

repeal: Take away

Important Jobs

Ben traveled back to Philadelphia in time to be a part of the First Continental Congress. He was one of the five men chosen to give **input** on the writing of the Declaration of Independence. Soon, however, he was sent back to Europe, this time to France, to try to raise financial support for the colonies.

> **input:** Advice

England had a strong navy and army. America was brand new and had none of those resources. They needed a friendly nation to help.

France and England were enemies and had fought each other during the French and Indian War in America years before. Ben persuaded the King of France to give financial help to the American colonial army. Many French officers went to America to help, including the Marquis de Lafayette. At the crucial time, King Louis even sent soldiers and part of his navy to help trap the English army at Yorktown, Virginia. With the help of the French and the mighty hand of God, America won her freedom, and the United States of America was born.

Constitutional Convention

Benjamin Franklin had tremendous influence at the Constitutional Convention, laying out a plan for governing the new nation. For four long months, through the oppressive heat of the summer of 1787, the members of the Convention sat day after day. There was much discussion by the members and disagreements about how to proceed. Ben suggested that they pray each day

Benjamin Franklin — Statesman, Inventor, and Patriot

to ask God's guidance in forming the nation. He said, "Sir, I have lived a long time, and the longer I live, the more convincing proofs I see of this truth, that God governs in the affairs of men. And if a sparrow cannot fall to the ground without his notice, is it probable that an empire can rise without His aid?"[5]

By this time, Ben Franklin was an old man of 81. He had a disease called gout in his feet that made it hard for him to stand. When he had something to say, he wrote it down and asked James Madison to read it for him. Some of those speeches he made were preserved in this way by Madison. One of the disputes was that the large states felt they should have the most say in the government. It was Franklin who helped settle the problem by suggesting that each state should have equal representation in the Senate, while in the House of Representatives, the membership should be according to the population.

When it came time for a vote, Franklin made a long speech that ended with: "On the whole sir, I cannot help expressing a wish that every member of the Convention who may still have objections to it, would, with me, on this occasion, doubt a little of his own **infallibility** and, to make manifest our **unanimity**, put his name to this instrument."[6]

infallibility: Inability to be wrong

unanimity: Agreement

While no one was satisfied with everything, in the end, most everyone did as Franklin suggested and put their names on the

Famous American Statesmen

document. Ben Franklin was cheerful and hopeful. After signing his name to the document, he stood watching the other members as they signed. He looked toward the president's chair where Washington sat to preside over the meeting. On its back was a picture of a half-risen sun. He commented, "I have often and often, in the course of the session and the **vicissitudes** of my hopes and fears as to its issue, looked at the sun behind the president without being able to tell whether it was rising or setting. But now, at length, I have the happiness to know that it is a rising, not a setting sun."[7] The United States of America began to take her place among the nations of the earth. Her light of liberty would shine brightly.

> **vicissitudes:**
> Negative changes

Benjamin Franklin — Statesman, Inventor, and Patriot

His Final Years

Franklin thought he would go home and enjoy farming, but the citizens of Pennsylvania had another idea. In 1787, they elected him for the third time as president of the Supreme Executive Council of Pennsylvania. Every citizen voted for him; Franklin was the only exception — he did not vote for himself. He answered the call to duty, however. He never accepted any pay for serving in that office. In 1788, he was elected as the president of the first anti-slavery society in America. When he was 84 years old, he wrote the first petition against slavery and submitted it to Congress. Franklin worked to the end of his life. His list of accomplishments is massive.

The last year of his life was spent mostly in his bed. Loved ones surrounded him. Friends wrote to him from all over the world. People visited him and made his life a pleasure despite his pain. At eleven o'clock on April 17, 1790, Benjamin Franklin died, with his eyes fixed on a picture of Christ, who he once said came to teach us to love one another. The whole world mourned for this gentleman, so loved and admired by all. He wrote his own **eulogy**: "The Body of B. Franklin, Printer, like the Cover of an old Book, Its Contents torn out, And stript of its Lettering and Gilding, Lies here, Food for Worms. But the Work shall not be **wholly** lost; For it will, as he believ'd appear once more, In a new & more perfect Edition, Corrected and amended By the Author. ~ Ben Franklin."[8]

eulogy: Something written about one who died

wholly: Completely

2

Samuel Adams –

Son of Liberty

Who Was Samuel Adams?

Sam Adams was one of America's founding fathers. As a writer, speaker, and statesman, he was a master at organizing and motivating others to take action. In this way, he was the driving force behind many events that led up to the War of Independence. Some call him the Father of the American Revolution.

Early Days

Samuel Adams was born on September 27, 1722, one of 12 children. His father was a **deacon** in Boston's Old South Church. His mother taught him to read and write. At six years old, he was able to read from the King James Bible. Sam's mother was a devoted Christian woman. Her teachings taken from the Bible guided Sam throughout his life.

deacon: A servant leader in the church

His family attended revival meetings, which were special gatherings where people came together to sing, pray, and listen to powerful messages about God. The ones they attended were led by Jonathan Edwards, who was a famous preacher of the revival called the Great Awakening during the mid-18th century.

Sam attended Boston Latin School for eight years and began his studies at Harvard College when he was 14. His parents wanted him to become a preacher, but he felt drawn to politics. To earn his master's degree, he wrote a paper explaining why people had the right to oppose leaders in order to preserve the common good.

Sam studied law for a while and then went to work for a Boston merchant. He was not a successful businessman, however. He simply had no interest in making money. Sam married his lifelong friend Elizabeth Checkley when he was 27. Elizabeth was an excellent wife. Unfortunately, of their six children, only two survived.

In 1756, he became a tax collector for the city of Boston. He failed at this job as well. He felt sorry for poor folks and would let them off without paying. Adams was always a friend to the poor. He ended up with little money and the town leaders wanted him to **cover** the amount he was short. He left that job and turned his time and attention to politics.

cover: Pay from his own money

He was elected to the Massachusetts House of Representatives and the Boston Town Meeting. These positions paid little, so he and his family had to live on a very small salary. Although Sam was poor, he was a man of integrity.

Troubles with England

Adams made friends with many of the people in Boston who opposed British rule. He wrote anti-British articles in a political newspaper. In 1764, the British Parliament passed the Sugar Act. It taxed molasses and other goods. Sam led protests against this act. He appealed to Britain to allow colonists to have representation in Parliament, but King George III

Samuel Adams — Son of Liberty

refused. Then the Stamp Act was passed in 1765. It taxed all printed documents. Sam felt something had to be done. He started the Sons of Liberty, a secret group that met to discuss how to deal with British tyranny. It soon spread to all 13 colonies.

In 1767, Britain passed the Townshend Acts. This law taxed paper, paint, lead, glass, and tea. Parliament used some of the money from taxes to maintain a small British army in America to force the colonists to comply with the new tax laws. The people of Boston refused to buy any British goods. This affected English merchants, who begged King George to repeal the tax. King George removed all taxes but the tax on tea. "There must be one tax to keep the right to tax," he reasoned.[9]

Sam Adams decided the colonists needed to communicate with each other. In 1772, at a Boston town meeting, he formed what he called a Committee of Correspondence. Its purpose was to create a system to exchange information with other Massachusetts towns. He wrote a letter encouraging other towns to do this as well, and within a few months there were 80 towns with their own committees. The colonists were working together now for a common cause. Adams spoke at the Committees of Correspondence to influence others. At one meeting, he read a report called, "The Rights of the Colonists." He believed the colonists had a natural right to life, liberty, and property. They also had the right to defend those things. Many of these ideas showed up later in the Declaration of Independence.

In 1773, Great Britain passed the Tea Act. Not only did they tax tea, but they forbade the colonists to buy tea from anyone except one British company, the East India Tea Company. This company sent ships full of British tea to America.

The Boston Tea Party

On a quiet Sunday morning, November 28, 1773, the ship *Dartmouth* sailed into Boston Harbor with instructions to unload its shipment of tea. Two other ships followed — the *Eleanor* and the *Beaver*. Sam called the Committee of Correspondence and 5,000 colonists together. He asked the group, "Is it the firm **resolution** of this body that the tea shall not only be sent back, but that no **duty** shall be paid thereon?"[10] It was a unanimous YES. Sam Adams and the people of Boston were firm that the tea should not be unloaded on American soil.

resolution: Decision

duty: Tax

Samuel Adams — Son of Liberty

Governor Thomas Hutchinson was equally determined that it should. According to law, the ships could not return to England with the tea without permission from either the governor or collector of customs. Neither of the men would yield an inch. The struggle continued for 19 days. Bostonians guarded the ships night and day with muskets and bayonets to be sure they were not unloaded. If they were, they would be forced to pay for it. If they were not landed by December 17, the revenue officer would be ordered to land them by force. Again, the colonists appealed to the governor and collector, but neither would give permission to send them back.

> **Governor Thomas Hutchinson:** The British-appointed governor of the colony of Massachusetts

On December 16, 1773, Sam Adams called upon the Sons of Liberty. They gathered at Boston Harbor dressed as Mohawk Native Americans, and walked down Milk Street toward Griffin's Wharf where the tea ships were anchored. The "Mohawks" boarded the ship, broke open 342 chests of tea, and poured the tea into Boston Harbor. There was no confusion and there was no violence. It was all very orderly. Then the men quietly returned to their homes.

King George's Punishment

When Parliament got the news about the "tea party," it passed a new set of laws as punishment. They were called the Intolerable Acts. First of all,

Boston's port was closed to all incoming or outgoing ships. Second, the king banned colonists from gathering at town meetings. Third, he demanded the colonists pay for the tea that had been destroyed. Fourth, he stationed British soldiers in Boston and forced colonists to **board** them.

Soldiers?! Stationed in homes in Boston?! This violated all the basic principles of the English constitution. The colonists were English citizens. Boston streets were swarming with soldiers in their red uniforms. Sam Adams trained his dog Queue to bark when he saw one of these redcoats. Something had to be done.

Adams sent the Committees of Correspondence into action and called for a meeting of representatives from all the colonies, to be held in Philadelphia in September of 1774. The meeting became known as the First Continental Congress. Many strong leaders from each colony attended. The gathering opened with a two-hour-long prayer meeting as the men called upon God to lead them and guide their proceedings. The colonies decided to support the Bostonians and brought them food and goods to share. They were in this together and would stick together.

board: Let them live in their homes

Lexington and Concord

British spies got word that the colonists had **stockpiled** ammunition in Lexington and Concord, Massachusetts. British General Gage received orders to seize the

stockpiled: Stored up

Samuel Adams — Son of Liberty

stores and also capture Samuel Adams and John Hancock, who were staying at the house of John Hancock's fiancée in Lexington. Boston patriots heard of the plot and Paul Revere, William Dawes, and Wentworth Cheswell were sent to warn the **minutemen**. They alerted Sam Adams and John Hancock of their danger. "As Adams and Hancock escaped across the fields together, the cracking of rifles reached their ears. 'Oh, what a glorious morning this is!'" said Adams.[11] He felt that it would eventually liberate the colony from the tyranny of Great Britain.

When British troops arrived at Lexington Green on the morning of April 19, 1775, they were met by Major John Pitcairn and his Lexington **militia**. A shot was fired, and in the battle that followed, eight Americans were killed. The British then marched on to Concord, only to find the countryside filled with militia who opened fire upon them. There was only one road back to Boston, and British officers realized the danger they were in. American sharpshooters hid behind trees and barns, and the red-coated British made easy targets.

> **minutemen:** Citizens ready to defend at a moment's notice
>
> **militia:** Citizen soldiers

At the end of the day, almost 300 British lay dead or wounded. The first battle of the War of Independence had been won by the American militia.

Second Continental Congress

The Second Continental Congress met in May 1775. The members declared war on Great Britain. While at the Second Continental Congress, Adams received troubling news. General Gage had said any American who would lay down his arms would be offered a pardon, except in the case of Sam Adams or John Hancock. They would not escape punishment. He also imposed martial law on the citizens of Boston, which meant there would be little freedom as 3,500 British soldiers flocked to enforce law in the city. Many residents were forced to flee as soldiers took over their homes. Sam Adams' house was occupied by Redcoats. The beloved Old South Meeting House was being used as a stable for British horses. Sam's son was trapped in the city. His wife and family had fled west to Watertown. His dear friend Joseph Warren had died in the Battle of Bunker Hill. Sam was saddened by the news, but it served to strengthen his resolve. Liberty was at stake.

Samuel Adams — Son of Liberty

The delegates decided they must write a document to explain their grievances to Great Britain and the world. Thomas Jefferson was selected to do most of the writing of the Declaration of Independence. It was issued on July 4, 1776. Members met in August to actually sign the document. Sam Adams gave a speech: "We have no alternative than independence. Courage, then, my countrymen, our contest is not only whether we ourselves shall be free, but whether there shall be left to mankind an **asylum** on earth for civil and religious liberty."[12] Stirred by his words, all 56 men added their names to the Declaration of Independence.

Articles of Confederation

Sam remained active in Congress with the many wartime decisions that had to be made. By the end of 1778, Adams wanted to retire from Congress and go home to his family. However, there was one last thing he wanted to see accomplished. He had helped to draft the Articles of Confederation in 1776–1777, which had functioned as the first agreement for the United States. On March 1, 1781, the Articles went into effect. Finally, after seven long years in Congress, Sam Adams started for home.

asylum: Safe place

The Boston he found was very different from the Boston he had left. Adams' home was now unlivable. He and his family moved into a house that had belonged to a **Tory**.

Sam Adams stayed active in Massachusetts affairs. Even while he was away at the Continental Congress, Sam had repeatedly been elected to the House of Representatives. He was elected to the Massachusetts Council. He also served as secretary of state. In 1779, he was selected to be on the committee writing the state's new constitution. In 1783, he was elected again to the Massachusetts Senate and chosen again as its president. It was the same year that the War of Independence was officially over and the United States was recognized as a nation among the countries of the world.

Tory: A colonist who was a British sympathizer

The Constitution of the United States

When the Constitution was written, it needed to be approved by each state. Sam Adams attended the ratifying convention in 1788. He opposed the new Constitution at first because he felt it did not give enough rights to individual people. He insisted on **amendments** to guarantee those rights. The Bill of Rights was added to the document. It guaranteed free speech and many other rights. Because of those amendments, Sam Adams approved it.

George Washington became the nation's first president. Sam's cousin, John Adams, was vice president. In 1789, Sam Adams became lieutenant governor of Massachusetts. His friend John Hancock was governor. Adams later became governor after John Hancock died.

amendments: Changes or additions

Sam was a strong advocate for states' rights. He did not want to see the federal government get too powerful.

Sam Adams retired from public life in 1797. He announced to the Massachusetts legislature, "The **infirmities** of age render me an unfit person in my own opinion, and probably in the opinion of others, to continue in this station."[13] Sam Adams had served the public for 40 years. He was 75 years old. He remained in Boston, enjoying time spent with family and old friends. His mind remained sound throughout his life, although his body became frail. His political **fervor** never **waned**. His final years were spent fighting for religious liberty.

infirmities: Illnesses

fervor: Passion

waned: Lessened

The great Samuel Adams died on October 3, 1803, in the presence of his beloved family. He had been influential in making the War of Independence a reality. He kept the people vigilant in defense of their liberties and drew attention to every act of tyranny. He sought to unify the colonies in the struggle for independence. Throughout his life, Adams fought to secure for the people the right to govern themselves. "Liberty was Adams' passion and liberty is his legacy."[14]

Famous American Statesmen

3

Patrick Henry –

The Voice of the Revolution

Who Was Patrick Henry?

Patrick Henry was a brilliant orator who greatly influenced others during the War of Independence with his moving speeches. He became known for his famous "Give Me Liberty or Give Me Death" speech. He also became the first governor of the Commonwealth of Virginia.

Early Years

Patrick Henry was born on May 29, 1736, to Sarah and John Henry in Hanover County, Virginia. He had a happy childhood. Patrick loved to be outdoors fishing, hunting, and swimming in the creek, and just enjoying the quietness of the woods. He loved listening to birds singing, and he imitated their songs. Watching the animals scamper about fascinated him. His parents faithfully taught him the Bible. Even though he loved reading the Bible, he did not enjoy school. This puzzled his father, who was a studious, scholarly man. Patrick would often skip school to go out to the woods.

Patrick's father, out of frustration, decided to teach him at home. Over the next five years, Patrick undertook a hard course of study. His family could not afford to send him to college, but he was well educated by his father. He learned Latin, Greek, mathematics, and history. When his parents saw he had a good ear for music, they got him a violin. He learned to fiddle on his own. As a teenager, he taught himself to play the harpsichord, lute, and flute, as well. He enjoyed music his whole life. Years later, when he had his own family, his children would sit in the parlor and sing hymns every Sunday evening. Patrick would accompany them on his violin.

Patrick was a quiet, thoughtful boy. When his friends had arguments, they would come to Patrick to find solutions. He would listen carefully to both sides and would take time to think about the situation while the boys' tempers cooled off. He then spoke to them calmly. Usually, both sides were happy with his decision. He seemed to have a natural ability to **sway** others through his words.

Patrick's First Job

When he was 15 years old, Patrick got a job as a clerk in the country store. Patrick worked there for a year. At his father's suggestion, when Patrick was 16, he and his brother William opened their own general store. Mr. Henry purchased a small house and helped his sons buy goods. They planned to pay their father back for his investment. They had plenty of customers, but they did not make a profit. They let

> **sway:** To influence or guide opinions

customers purchase items on credit. Patrick always felt sorry for those who could not pay.

Patrick enjoyed listening to his customers, especially those talking about politics. He had read so much and was so **articulate** that many times, people who came into the store defending King George III left with a different opinion. Patrick's words and passion changed their minds.

> **articulate:** Able to express thoughts clearly

After a year, it was clear they would have to close the store. Mr. Henry declared that Patrick seemed doomed to failure. He was no more successful at storekeeping than he had been at school. Patrick had other interests besides the store, though. He was 18 years old, and he fell in love. He proposed to Sarah Shelton, who was 16 years old. Their parents did not like the idea of their marriage at first but soon gave their consent. Sarah's parents gave the couple 300 acres of land and a manor house at Pine Slash. In a year, a baby girl was born to them.

Patrick worked hard at farming, but because of **drought** and poor soil conditions, his efforts were unsuccessful. Three years after Patrick and Sarah married, the house at Pine Slash caught

> **drought:** Not enough rain

fire and burned to the ground. The young family had to move in with Sarah's parents. Two more children were born to Patrick and Sarah. For a while, Patrick helped his father-in-law run his inn, Hanover Tavern. It was a tremendous opportunity for him to meet many Virginians.

One day, Patrick and Sarah were invited to a party at the home of Colonel Dandridge, a planter and clerk of New Kent County, Virginia. Patrick was pleasant and carried on conversations with all the guests. Here, he met Thomas Jefferson and learned that Jefferson was studying law. On their way home, Patrick told Sarah he would like to study law, too. Even though he had failed at so many things, she believed in him. She told him she knew he could do whatever he wanted to.

Patrick Becomes a Lawyer

Sarah proved to be right; Patrick was determined to be a lawyer, so he devoted himself to studying law. He was blessed with an excellent memory, a quick wit, and a talent for knowing what was important. He was a devoted reader of the Bible, which greatly influenced his **perspective**. Patrick spent the next six weeks studying nonstop. Then he kissed Sarah and the children and headed off for Williamsburg to get a license to practice law.

perspective: Attitude and speech

Patrick Henry — The Voice of the Revolution

He went to the College of William and Mary to find his friend Thomas Jefferson. Tom was surrounded by books. He was astonished when Patrick told him he had come to apply for his law license so soon. At first, the lawyers who administered the test did not want to give him a chance, but after a few hours of discussion and debate, John Randolph exclaimed, "Mr. Henry, if your **industry** be half equal to your genius, I know you will become … an honor to your profession."[15] Patrick Henry was excited as he rode home that April afternoon. He could hardly wait to tell Sarah. After 24 years of failure, he was finally on the right path. He had discovered what God had gifted him to do.

Patrick Henry — The Parson's Cause

During his first year as a lawyer, Patrick served 60 clients. In any fight, he favored the **underdog**. Patrick liked all people and believed in them. He had the gift of influencing the way others thought. Patrick had become a hardworking, dependable attorney. By the end of three

> **industry:** Hard work
>
> **underdog:** One who was at a disadvantage

Famous American Statesmen

years, he was sufficiently supporting his family, which had now grown to five children. He even gave some financial support to his mother and father.

One of Patrick's first cases involved an **altercation** between ministers of the Church of England and the local government. He argued against the ministers and in favor of the colonists. As he spoke, a deathlike silence fell in the courtroom. "The people passed a law and the preachers persuaded the king to set it aside. These preachers have failed in their duties. They have become enemies of the people."[16] His speech **undermined** the state church and put royal authority in question. In a one-hour speech, Patrick Henry became the people's hero.

altercation: An angry dispute

undermined: Made weaker

House of Burgesses

The people of Louisa County loved Patrick Henry. When a vacancy opened in the House of Burgesses, people who represented the colonists, they elected him as their delegate. That spring, Patrick returned to Williamsburg. He had been a delegate for nine days. It was a Wednesday, May 29, 1765, his 29th birthday. The month-long session

Patrick Henry — The Voice of the Revolution

of the House was drawing to a close. Some members had already left for home. Only 39 of the 116 Burgesses were present.

George Johnson of Fairfax County made a motion that the members consider the Stamp Act, a tax recently imposed on the colonies by King George III. Quickly, Patrick Henry jumped to his feet to second the motion. Could this be done? The Stamp Act had already been passed by Parliament, the legitimate British governing body with legal authority to tax the colonies. Nevertheless, the House of Burgesses took a vote, and the motion **carried**.

Patrick knew he must wait his turn to speak since he was a new member. George Wythe reminded the delegates that they had appealed to King George the previous November, and the king had refused to listen. Patrick Henry believed that Virginia could not just submit without protest. He slowly rose from his chair, first captivating his audience with a bit of humor. Then, he opened his book and presented his seven resolutions. The point of these resolutions was to prove that the Virginia Assembly had the **sole** right to lay taxes on the colony; to speak otherwise made one an

> **carried:** Would be heard

> **sole:** Only

36 Famous American Statesmen

enemy of the colony. There was a dread stillness in the room over this issue, followed by a **contentious** debate.

Famous Speech

Once again, Patrick Henry rose. He spoke with passion as his rich voice sent chills through his listeners. They were hearing one of the most famous **orations** in the history of our country. "Caesar had his Brutus, Charles the First his Cromwell, and George the Third…."[17]

The speaker yelled, "Treason!" Followers of King George yelled, "Treason!" Henry paused dramatically. It seemed as if the Burgesses were frozen in place, totally **mesmerized**. Emphasizing each word, Henry slowly finished his sentence: "And George the Third may profit by their example."[18] Thomas Jefferson later praised Henry's oration as being greater than he ever heard from any other man. The time for voting had arrived. Henry's resolution won — by one vote! Those who had voted against him stormed out of the room. Others ran to congratulate him. George Washington approached Henry and said, "Mr. Henry, today you have put Virginia first."[19]

contentious: Quarrelsome

orations: Formal speeches

mesmerized: Fascinated

Patrick Henry — The Voice of the Revolution

News of Henry's speech spread to the other colonies and across the Atlantic to England. Americans began to **boycott** English goods. William Pitt, a British orator in Parliament, said, "I rejoice that America has resisted. My position is this. I will maintain it to my last hour: no taxation without representation."[20] On March 18, 1766, Parliament repealed the dreaded Stamp Act. There was rejoicing in England as well as America. Patrick Henry was re-elected to the House of Burgesses. Tom Jefferson was now the delegate from Albemarle County, Virginia. He said to Patrick, "To me, a patriot is a man who gives his first love and loyalty to the land of his birth. It's an American rather than an English word, Pat, and you're a perfect example of it."[21]

> **boycott:** Refuse to buy

Give Me Liberty or Give Me Death

The conflict between the king and the colonies continued to grow. The colonists in Boston protested the tax on tea, demonstrating their anger by taking part in the Boston Tea Party. In **retaliation**, King George III closed the port of Boston. Delegates throughout the other colonies met and voted to band together to help their fellow colonists in Boston. In Virginia, Patrick Henry, of course, spoke persuasively on the matter. Not once did Henry waver from his course.

> **retaliation:** To get revenge

Famous American Statesmen

George Washington stood ready to serve his country. Thomas Jefferson had his pen **poised** to aid in the struggle, but it was Patrick Henry who served as the Voice of the Revolution. Patrick Henry blazed the trail for liberty.

The **crowning glory** of Patrick Henry's oratory took place on March 23, 1775. Henry was 39 years old. The Second Virginia Convention met at St. John's Episcopal Church in Richmond, Virginia. One hundred and twenty delegates, the finest Virginia leaders, were packed into the pews. The meeting had been called because the king and Parliament refused to pay any attention to the petitions sent by the Continental Congress. King George had sent his answer in the form of warships and an army with instructions to General Gage to punish the colonists if they did not obey the king's orders.

poised: Ready

crowning glory: Greatest achievement

Patrick Henry wanted to persuade the Virginia delegates that they must prepare for war. Others were talking about avoiding war. Henry felt the time had passed to avoid war. Arguments grew heated. At last, Patrick Henry rose to speak. He started calmly, but as he spoke, the delegates saw his eyes flash. His voice was full of passion.

"We have done everything we could to avert the storm that is now coming on…. If we wish to be free, we must fight. I repeat it, sir, we

Patrick Henry — The Voice of the Revolution

must fight…. The battle, sir, is not to the strong alone. It is to the vigilant, the active, the brave. It is now too late to **retire** from the contest. There is no retreat but in submission and slavery. Our chains are **forged**. Their clanking may be heard on the plains of Boston. The war is **inevitable**. And let it come! I repeat, sir, let it come! Gentlemen may cry peace, peace, but there is no peace. Our **brethren** are already in the field. Why stand we here idle? What is it the gentlemen wish? What would they have? Is life so dear, or peace so sweet, as to be purchased at the price of chains and slavery?"[22]

At this point, Patrick Henry lowered his head and crossed his wrists to resemble chains upon his arms, as a prisoner in **agony**. He paused, then raised his eyes toward heaven and prayed, "Forbid it, Almighty God!"[23] He turned to the Loyalists and slowly bent toward the ground, his hands still crossed. He appeared to be a slave, weighed down with chains. "I know not what course others may take, but as for me, give me liberty…."[24] As he slowly pronounced each syllable of "liberty," he acted as if his chains were breaking. He opened his arms and raised his hands. He stood tall and straight, **personifying** a free man, "… or give me death!"[25]

As he cried out the word "death," he acted as if he were driving a dagger into his heart. The

---

retire: Withdraw

forged: Beat into shape

inevitable: Unavoidable

brethren: Those loved like family

agony: Pain

personifying: Acting like

Famous American Statesmen

effect was **electrifying**. Peyton Randolph, one of the delegates present, explained, "Henry's passion melted us into one mass. As soon as the convention voted to arm Virginia, it was clear his words were not just words, but action."[26]

Faithful Till the End

The wonderful speech moved not only Virginians, but all the colonies and the world. The war officially began the following month with the Battle of Lexington and Concord. Shortly thereafter, Patrick Henry was appointed commander-in-chief of Virginia's military forces. Later still, he was elected Governor of Virginia for five **successive** terms. He remained a leading force in America's War of Independence.

Patrick Henry retired from public office at the age of 58. He lived with his family at Red Hill, an estate he owned in Charlotte County, Virginia. Here, he lived a simple life surrounded by amazing trees and breathtaking scenery in his beloved Virginia. He died of stomach cancer on June 6, 1799.

electrifying: Thrilling

successive: Back to back

His impassioned speech played a vitally important role in shaping the course of events that resulted in the War of Independence. He truly deserves the title: *The Voice of the Revolution*.

4

John Hancock –
Dedicated Patriot

January 12, 1737 – October 8, 1793

Who Was John Hancock?

John Hancock was one of the founding fathers of our country. He presided over the Continental Congress and signed the Declaration of Independence. He was a statesman, merchant, and governor of Massachusetts.

Early Days

John Hancock was born on January 12, 1737, to John and Mary Hancock in Braintree, a small town near Boston, Massachusetts. When John was born, Massachusetts was a colony of Great Britain. They called Great Britain their "mother country." John's father was pastor of the North Church in Braintree. John was the second of three children. Interestingly, Reverend John, his father, had baptized John Adams. The young John Adams and John Hancock were friends.

John's father died when he was just seven years old. Mrs. Hancock was left with three children to raise. She had a hard time making ends meet. John's uncle, Thomas Hancock, stepped up to help her. He was a **merchant** and owned many ships. His ships sailed from Massachusetts to London, England, transporting goods such as timber, furs, and fish.

> **merchant:** A person who buys and sells goods

Famous American Statesmen

Uncle Thomas was a wealthy man. He and his wife had no children. They invited John to live with them in Boston. Thomas had built one of the grandest mansions in Boston for himself and his wife on Beacon Hill. They sent John to the Boston Latin School, the oldest public school in America. Thomas bought him fine clothes to wear. When he graduated from school in 1750, John enrolled in Harvard College. Thomas and his father before him had graduated from Harvard. Here, John learned about **theology** and classical literature. When John finished school, he went to work for his uncle in the mercantile business.

> **theology:** The study of God and His relation to the world

Becoming a Merchant

Thomas Hancock's shipping business prospered during the French and Indian War. Thomas had close contacts with the royal governors of Massachusetts. This enabled him to get government contracts to supply muskets, shot, powder, uniforms, and other military equipment to the British forces and the colonial militia. Such items were needed to fight the war. John learned much about his uncle's business during the war. Thomas sent

John to England in 1760. He encouraged John to build relationships with his customers and suppliers. John lived there for a year, and reading the correspondence between John and his uncle, it is clear that John was successful in his **endeavor**.

When John returned to Boston, he found Uncle Thomas was in poor health. During the next two years, Thomas turned many of his business responsibilities over to John. In January 1763, he made John a partner. John joined many organizations in Boston, and through these, he met Paul Revere, Dr. Joseph Warren, and other Patriots.

endeavor: Effort

John's uncle died in 1764, when John was 27 years old. John inherited his uncle's business, his house on Beacon Hill, and thousands of acres. He was now one of the richest men in Massachusetts. John prospered, as many colonists needed items made in England, and people in England needed things the colonists produced. John was wealthy, but he was also a very generous man. He gave food and firewood to the poor and contributed great sums to the churches of Boston. John had many friends because he was so kind to others.

Trouble with England

Britain had won the French and Indian War, but in doing so had acquired much debt. King George III decided to tax his colonies to try to make up for some of his financial losses. The colonists did not see that the war had done much to help them. They fought, of course, but the victory served to extend the kingdom of King George; it didn't really improve life for the colonists. There were no representatives from the colonies in Parliament, and therefore, legally, Parliament had no right to tax them. It was an abuse of their rights as English citizens.

The Sugar Act of 1764 directly affected John Hancock and his fellow merchants. Molasses was taxed, and the collection of taxes became stricter. Boston merchants were already suffering from a post-war **depression** of trade. They felt this was a direct **assault** on their rights. They appealed to the king to repeal the Sugar Act. Sam Adams and James Otis got 50 successful Boston merchants to agree not to import English goods as a protest.

> **depression:** Economic loss
>
> **assault:** Attack

The Stamp Act of 1765

Instead of repealing the Sugar Act, King George added the Stamp Act to the colonists' burden. This act required every paper document in the colonies to bear a stamp that proved they had paid tax on it. This tax affected almost every colonist's daily life. The colonists convened a special meeting called the Stamp Act Congress. The members of Congress called for a boycott on English goods. In March 1765, John Hancock was elected as one of Boston's five

selectmen. His uncle had previously held this post for many years. At first, as a selectman, John felt the colonists must **submit** to the Stamp Act. "I am heartily sorry for the great burden laid upon us, we are not able to bear all things, but must submit to the higher powers, these taxes will greatly affect us, our Trade will be ruined, and as it is, it's very dull."[27]

selectmen: The ruling body of a town

submit: Willingly obey

entreaty: A plea or petition

detrimental: Damaging

He changed his mind, however, when the dreaded stamps arrived from England a month later. He wrote an **entreaty**, appealing to Britain as the mother country. He laid out the **detrimental** effects the stamps would have on the colonists and England alike. Hancock had attended a town hall meeting 18 days before he wrote the letter. As a selectman, he had been chosen to write instructions for the representatives in the Massachusetts General Assembly concerning how to respond to the Stamp Act crisis.

John Hancock did not protest actively, although many others led protests and hung anti-Stamp Act posters throughout the town. English citizens pleaded with King George to repeal the act because the boycott was affecting their income. Word reached the colonies in May 1766 that the Stamp Act had finally been repealed. There was rejoicing in the streets of Boston. John Hancock was elected to the Massachusetts House of Representatives that same month.

More Taxes

In 1767, Parliament passed new laws called the Townshend Acts. Merchants owning ships had even higher taxes to pay. The colonists felt these laws were not just, because they violated their rights as English citizens. **Commodities** like glass, paper, and tea were now taxed. To make matters worse, the money collected was used to pay the British governors and judges, whose job was to enforce the new laws. Parliament also created the American Customs Board to discover and prevent merchants from sneaking their ships into port to avoid paying taxes.

Even merchants who had never **smuggled** goods into the colonies were in opposition to the oppressive rules. Again, the colonists wrote, appealing to Parliament and King George. John, as selectman, authored the letter. It was a polite letter, carefully explaining the problems the Townshend Acts created and asking to have them revoked. Instead, John Hancock was **targeted** by the customs board.

On April 9, 1768, two customs employees boarded one of John's ships and accused John of not paying taxes on his cargo. They did not have a search warrant, which was an official paper giving them authority to search his ship.

commodities: Economic goods

smuggled: Brought in illegally

targeted: Made an object of attack

John Hancock — Dedicated Patriot

John Hancock refused to let them go below deck without the proper warrant. The customs officials wanted to file charges against John, but dropped the case when Massachusetts Attorney General Jonathan Sewall investigated and found no laws had been broken by Hancock or his men.

On May 9, another of Hancock's ships, the *Liberty*, arrived in port with cargo. Customs officers inspected the ship and counted the goods. John paid the tax. They claimed there was extra space on the ship and accused John of having smuggled goods ashore before they counted his inventory. They had no evidence of this. He was informed that England was **seizing** his ship. It would no longer belong to him. John wanted to get his ship back, but he would not pay unlawful taxes to do it. The British then used John's ship to enforce trade regulations.

In October, John was ordered to appear in court. He was charged with not paying taxes on his cargo. John Adams represented him as his attorney. The court had no jury, and the judge refused to let Adams **cross-examine** witnesses. The trial lasted five long months; then without explanation, the charges against John Hancock were suddenly dropped. The

seizing: Taking for oneself

cross-examine: Ask questions of

people of Boston were up in arms over what had happened to John Hancock, their generous friend. King George sent four regiments of British troops to Boston to **occupy** the city after the *Liberty* incident.

Sons of Liberty

Sam Adams had just started a group called the Sons of Liberty, colonists who banded together to decide what to do about troubles with England. The Sons of Liberty asked Bostonians not to buy English tea. Bostonian women began to make tea from berries or leaves instead. A meeting was called in September to decide what to do about British troops flooding their city. They agreed to send a letter to King George again, telling him there was no need for troops in Boston. They were loyal, peaceful British subjects who only wanted their voices heard. Their charter with England did not allow troops to be stationed without the consent of the citizens. When their appeal was ignored, Sam Adams, the voice of the people, stepped in and said, "Where law ends, tyranny begins!"[28]

occupy: Live in and police

Parliament passed the Tea Act of 1773, preventing the colonists from buying tea from any merchant except the

East India Tea Company, which was owned by England. Bostonians tried to stop the tea from being unloaded and told the ships to sail back to England. They would not be forced to pay for the unwanted tea. However, the ships could not sail back without the direct order of British Governor Hutchinson, and he would not give his permission.

The colonists ended up dumping the tea into the harbor, and this made King George furious when he found out. Although John Hancock had not participated in dumping the tea, the king was sure that Sam Adams and John Hancock were **instigators**. Now the English came up with a plan.

Lexington and Concord

The English learned that the colonists were stockpiling ammunition in Lexington and Concord. They planned a raid on those towns to **confiscate** it. British General Gage also gave orders to arrest John Hancock and Sam Adams. They were both staying in the Hancock-Clarke house in Lexington. General Gage wanted them sent to London to be tried

instigators: Persons behind an uprising

confiscate: Take possession of

Famous American Statesmen

and possibly hung. Paul Revere was dispatched to warn the colonists, Adams, and Hancock of the British raid. Hancock and Adams discussed their next move. Hancock wanted to stay and fight, but Adams convinced him his leadership was needed; the colonists could not afford to lose John Hancock. They escaped just in the nick of time. When the **"shot heard round the world"** rang out, the War of Independence began.

As noted before, General Gage issued a proclamation granting a **pardon** to any colonist who "would lay down their arms and return to the duties of peaceable subjects" except for Sam Adams and John Hancock.[29] Those two would not be pardoned.

> **shot heard round the world:** First shot fired on Lexington Green

> **pardon:** Release from punishment

Second Continental Congress

Now that war was declared, John Hancock and other delegates started off for the meeting of the Second Continental Congress in Philadelphia, Pennsylvania. On May 24, 1775, Hancock was **unanimously** elected president of the Continental Congress. During a recess

> **unanimously:** Without opposition

John Hancock — Dedicated Patriot

of Congress, John and his fiancée, Dorothy Quincy, were married. They would later have two children.

By the summer of 1776, the colonies decided they must declare their independence from Great Britain. Five men were chosen to be on a committee responsible for drafting the document stating their intentions. Congress approved the document on July 2, 1776. It underwent a few revisions, so July 4, 1776, became the official Independence Day. John Hancock was still serving as president of the Continental Congress when the Declaration of Independence was signed. President Hancock was the first man to sign. He signed his name in extra-large letters. He said he wrote it that way so that King George would not need his glasses to be able to read it. All 56 men who signed the document knew that if they were caught by the British, they would be punished. John knew he would lose all his ships, his money, and possibly his life if he were caught.

Back to Boston

John requested a leave from Congress in October. He wanted to return home, but the people needed him in the local government and re-elected him to the House of Representatives. He was very generous to the citizens of Boston. He helped support the women and children who had become widows and orphans due to the war. In 1778, he was made senior major general of the Massachusetts militia and led men into battle.

Hancock continued to serve the people. In 1780, he was elected governor, winning more than 90% of the vote. He remained governor throughout the war, although he resigned for a brief time in 1785 for health reasons. He was suffering from gout, a type of arthritis causing episodes of severe pain. He was re-elected governor in 1787, and remained in that office, serving the state of Massachusetts for nine terms, until the end of his life. He died at his home on October 8, 1793. He was only 56 years old. His friend Sam Adams replaced him as governor and declared the day of Hancock's burial a state holiday. The people of Massachusetts gave a stately **interment** to the man who had risked his great fortune to help obtain "life, liberty, and the pursuit of happiness" for all Americans.

> **interment:** Burial

5

Alexander Hamilton –
Designer of American Government

January 11, 1757 – July 12, 1804

Who Was Alexander Hamilton?

Alexander Hamilton was one of America's founding fathers. He fought in the War of Independence, helped draft the Constitution, and served as the first Secretary of the Treasury. He was the chief **architect** of our American financial system.

The Early Years

Alexander Hamilton was born on January 11, 1757, on a small island in the West Indies. It was a British colony. Alexander and his brother James had lots of books. They loved playing on the sandy beaches and climbing the palm trees growing on the island, and were both tutored by their mother. Alexander especially enjoyed English, writing, and poetry. Their early childhood was happy and peaceful. Their father, James, moved the family to the island of St. Croix in 1765. Life there was harder.

architect: Designer

When Alexander was 11 years old, his father, under financial hardship, left to go to another island looking for better work. Alexander never saw him again. His mother opened a store, and Alexander and James helped her work there.

Famous American Statesmen

After a year, both Alexander and his mother got very sick with a high fever. Alexander recovered, but his mother died. James and Alexander went to live with an adult cousin, but in just a few years, the adult cousin died. The two boys were alone in the world.

Jobs

James went to work for a carpenter on St. Croix. Alexander went to work for a merchant who had five children of his own. Ned, one of the merchant's sons, was a year older than Alexander. They became good friends. At 13 years old, Alexander got a job as a clerk in a **mercantile house**. As part of his job, he learned to handle money and order supplies. He was very skilled in mathematics. However, Alexander did not want to do this job forever.

Ned was leaving for New York to go to medical school. Alexander wanted to do something significant with his life. He did not have enough money to travel, nor did he know if travel would be necessary. He had dreams of perhaps being a great soldier.

In August 1772, a terrible hurricane hit St. Croix and caused major destruction. Alexander wrote a story describing the hurricane using **vivid** language. It was published in St. Croix's paper, *The Gazette*. The article impressed some wealthy residents.

mercantile house: A business that shipped goods all over the world

vivid: Highly descriptive

Thinking Alexander had great potential, they took up a collection and raised enough money to send him to school in New York.

New York

Ned was waiting for him when he arrived. Alexander enrolled in Elizabethtown Academy in New Jersey. Here he studied Latin, Greek, and math for six months to prepare him for college. Then he enrolled in King's College in New York, now Columbia University. He enjoyed college and got along well with his roommates. He surprised his roommates by getting down on his hands and knees every morning and night to pray.

All over town, there was constant talk of the troubles with England. At first, Alexander was not sure whether he should side with the Tories or the **Patriots**. He determined to study the issue. In the end, he gave a passionate speech explaining his quickly growing **allegiance** to the Patriots. People who heard his speech were stunned at his persuasiveness and **oratory**. Politics became Alexander's new passion. He spoke at rallies and published articles for newspapers. Audiences listened to

Patriots: The colonists committed to freedom

allegiance: Commitment

oratory: Speaking skills

Alexander with **rapt** attention. But Alexander never finished college because the War of Independence began in April 1775.

Commissioned

In early 1776, 21-year-old Alexander Hamilton was **commissioned** as captain of the New York Provincial Company of Artillery. Captain Hamilton was responsible for **recruiting** men and supplying them with uniforms. He demanded that his soldiers be well trained, disciplined, and well **outfitted**. On July 2, 1776, delegates to the Continental Congress voted to approve the Declaration of Independence. On the same day, Alexander watched a great fleet of British ships sail into New York harbor. They were full of British soldiers and **Hessian mercenaries**. On July 9, General Washington and his soldiers stood in the **Commons** just below King's College to hear the Declaration of Independence read to the troops. The colonies now felt like a free and independent country. Everyone cheered as soldiers fired 13 rounds, one for each of the 13 states. Alexander Hamilton was excited, but he knew trouble was ahead.

rapt: Wholly absorbed

commissioned: Given the rank

recruiting: Signing up

outfitted: Dressed

Hessian: German

mercenaries: Soldiers hired for money

Commons: Park

The Business of War

Alexander fought alongside General Washington at the Battle of White Plains in October 1776. On December 25, Washington planned his surprise attack on the Hessians at Trenton. Alexander was very ill at that time, but got out of bed and led his 68 men on an eight-mile march through snow to join Washington. Alexander showed his men respect, and they respected him in return. He and his men fought admirably and soundly defeated the Hessians. Washington later commented on Alexander's performance in the battle, saying he was "charmed by the brilliant courage and admirable skill of the young officer."[30]

A few weeks later, General Washington asked Alexander Hamilton to be his assistant. At first, Alexander hesitated. He really enjoyed fighting on the battlefield. As he thought it over, however, it was too good an opportunity to miss. His job included writing letters to the Continental Congress and senior officers. He would inform them of the latest news and request needed items. He also attended meetings at which Washington could not be present. Though only 21 years old, he was now a lieutenant colonel. Hamilton became fast friends with Marquis de Lafayette, who was only 19 years old. Alexander spoke French, so he often translated Lafayette's words for General Washington.

These three men fought together at the Battle of Monmouth on June 28, 1778. The battle proved to be fierce. Alexander had his horse shot out from under him and had to be carried off the field. Fortunately, as the day drew to a close, the British retreated. Washington, Hamilton, and Lafayette were reunited.

Alexander was in Morristown, New Jersey, in the winter of 1780. Here he met Elizabeth "Eliza" Schuyler. She was the daughter of a famous, brave general, Philip Schuyler. Eliza had come to Morristown to visit her aunt. She was immediately attracted to Alexander, and the couple was married in November. Alexander was warmly welcomed into the Schuyler family. After so many years, Alexander finally had a family he could call his own.

Plans and Plots

In his spare time, Alexander Hamilton began recording his thoughts about how a new government should be organized. Two big questions were: how could it repay the debt it incurred due to the war, and how should it organize public finances? He wrote a 6,000-word **proposal** to a member of Congress. Hamilton was a strong **proponent** of a national bank owned equally by the government and private **investors**. The bank would be able to print money and make loans. He felt the country would have to borrow large sums from foreign countries. That was how France and Britain raised money during wartime. He studied how other countries operated and contemplated different options.

Hamilton was eating breakfast one day with Major General Benedict Arnold. Hamilton was unaware that Arnold was a **traitor**. Arnold planned to turn the command of **West Point** over to the British on the very day he

proposal: Plan

proponent: Supporter

investors: People who put money into something expecting to make a profit

traitor: A betrayer of one's country

West Point: The well-known school that trains military leaders

was having breakfast with Alexander Hamilton. While dining, Arnold received a **dispatch** that plans had gone wrong. He rushed out of the house to the river, boarded a boat, and got away. Hamilton went in search of him when he finally learned of the plot, but Arnold had the advantage of time and escaped.

A Soldier Again

Hamilton decided to stop working as **aide-de-camp** for General Washington in early 1781. He missed being a soldier. That summer, Washington sent him to Yorktown, Virginia, to take command. There, he joined the 17,000 French and Continental soldiers to fight the Battle of Yorktown. October 14, 1781, was a very dark night. Alexander thought of a plan. He wanted to attack the British soldiers with a surprise nighttime strike. He had his men use only bayonets so the noise of guns would not alert the unsuspecting British troops. In less than ten minutes, Alexander and his men forced the British to surrender and helped win the war! Newspapers all over the country published the story of Alexander's victory. He finally had achieved his dream of long ago, and became a **distinguished** soldier.

dispatch: Notice

aide-de-camp: Confidential assistant

distinguished: Excellent

Famous American Statesmen

Home Again

Alexander missed his wife very much. He returned home in January 1782, just in time for the birth of their first child, Philip Hamilton. Alexander decided to leave the military and become a lawyer, so he could spend time with his family. He also wanted time to help guide the new nation. After studying law for six months, Alexander passed the bar exam and got his law license. He moved the family to New York City to open his practice. While studying law, he agreed to become the federal tax collector for the state of New York. It proved to be an **arduous** job. Many New Yorkers did not want to pay taxes to the federal government. Instead, they felt money should stay in their own state.

> **arduous:** Hard, difficult

Alexander Hamilton was chosen as a delegate to the Congress of the Confederation, the governing body of the United States under the Articles of Confederation before the Constitution was written and adopted. He and James Madison wrote *The Federalist Papers*, a collection of articles and essays discussing possible solutions for how to organize the new government. *The Federalist Papers* outlined three branches of government. (1) The Executive Branch, headed by the president, would enforce the laws. (2) Congress, the Legislative

Alexander Hamilton—Designer of American Government

Branch, would be responsible for making the laws. (3) A Supreme Court would be the Judicial Branch, making decisions on the constitutionality of the laws. This structure allowed for checks and balances among the branches, so no one branch would have too much power. When the Constitution was finally written, many of its ideas were based on Alexander Hamilton's and James Madison's 85 *Federalist Papers.*

The Constitutional Convention

Fifty-five delegates from all the individual states met together for the Constitutional Convention from May 25 until September 17, 1787. Their job was to write a new Constitution, a document that would govern the new nation. It had to be agreed upon by at least nine out of the 13 states. The country was beginning to fall into two groups. People who believed in a strong and central federal government were called Federalists. Those who wanted to see more power left in the hands of the states were called Anti-Federalists. These included men such as Thomas Jefferson and James Madison. They finally agreed after much debate, writing, and rewriting. The Constitution became law on June 21, 1788. George Washington became president on April 30, 1789.

Thirty-four-year-old Alexander Hamilton was appointed **Secretary of the Treasury**. He would help decide how to set up monetary systems for the United States, something he had been thinking about for quite a while. Alexander gladly accepted the position and quit his law practice to focus on his new role. He was eager to serve his country. He held this office until 1795.

Secretary of the Treasury: The president's cabinet member that advises on economic and money matters

Many people disagreed with Alexander's idea of setting up one bank for the entire nation. They were afraid it would benefit only wealthy people. President Washington agreed with Hamilton, and finally, Hamilton convinced Congress to establish the nation's first bank.

Alexander gave up his government job in 1795 to spend more time with his family. He reopened his law office. He and his wife now had six children. After leaving office, Alexander took a three-week tour, meeting with Native American people in New York. He had often used his influence in government to protect their rights.

Alexander Hamilton—Designer of American Government

He helped manage a school that taught them both English and Native American languages. President Washington retired from office in 1796. Knowing Alexander's skill with words, he asked Alexander Hamilton to write his Farewell Address. The speech was published and **circulated** in newspapers all over the country.

The Yellow Fever

In 1798, New York City was hit with a yellow fever **epidemic**. People thought that poor water quality was adding to the severity of the epidemic. Aaron Burr, an employee of the state of New York, proposed laying pipes to bring fresh water to New Yorkers. Hamilton supported his plan, thinking it was a good idea. In truth, though, Burr raised money by telling people it was for clean water, but he planned to keep part of the money for himself and the organizers of the project. Using the water project as an excuse, Aaron Burr also created another bank from which he could borrow whenever he wished. He and his Manhattan Company raised $2 million, but only $100,000 was actually used to provide water for the city. People kept getting sick. Alexander Hamilton was furious when he discovered what was happening. He considered Aaron Burr a dishonest man, and was not happy when Burr was chosen as vice president in 1801.

circulated: Passed around

epidemic: Widespread disease outbreak

After his term as vice president was up, Aaron Burr ran for governor of New York in 1804. Hamilton supported Burr's opponent. When Burr lost, he put part of the blame on Hamilton. At a dinner at a friend's house, Hamilton told a friend that he distrusted Burr. Another dinner guest wrote to his brother, telling him that Hamilton had called Burr untrustworthy. Somehow, the letter was published in the newspaper. Aaron Burr demanded an apology. Alexander refused. Burr challenged Hamilton to a **duel**. In the 1700s, when men disagreed and couldn't solve their problems by talking, they would duel using guns. Usually, both duelers would fire into the air to show the end of their disagreement, not actually shoot at each other.

> **duel:** A combat with weapons fought between two persons in the presence of witnesses

An Unfortunate End

Hamilton did not tell his family about the duel. He finished up his law cases and he told a few close friends that he would not fire at Burr. He wrote goodbye letters to his family in case he did not survive. The duel was set for seven o'clock on July 11, 1804. Each man was allowed one other man to accompany him, and a doctor was present as well. Each man had a flintlock pistol. The two men raised their guns. When the proper signal was given, Alexander shot into the air, hitting a tree. Burr shot Alexander above the hip. Alexander fell to the ground. Dr. Hosack ran to Alexander and rushed him to the

Alexander Hamilton—Designer of American Government

house of a friend. Soon his entire family was by his bedside. By the next afternoon, Alexander Hamilton was dead.

Every business in New York closed on the day of his funeral. The New York Supreme Court draped its bench with black fabric for the rest of the term. Eliza was too upset to attend the funeral. Alexander had written her a letter that ended with, "Adieu best of wives and best of women. Embrace my darling children for me."[31]

Many New Yorkers were very upset and thought Aaron Burr should be arrested, but he never was. He always referred to Alexander after the event as, "my friend Hamilton — whom I shot."[32] People were shocked at how little emotion he showed about it. Someone even threatened to burn down his house. His reputation was ruined, and he finally fled New York and moved to Philadelphia.

Alexander Hamilton's great influence is still felt today. We continue to rely on the national banking system he established. The Bank of New York that he founded is still in existence, the oldest bank in the country. Alexander Hamilton's picture began appearing on the ten-dollar bill in 1928. *The Federalist Papers* that he and James Madison wrote are the basis for how our government is to be run and are quoted by Supreme Court justices in cases today. Through his hard work, his dream of doing something important certainly came true.

6

Henry Clay –
The Great Peacemaker

April 12, 1777 – June 29, 1852

Who Was Henry Clay?

Henry Clay was an American lawyer and statesman. He used his skill in delivering persuasive speeches to bring about peace in government. He served as Secretary of State under John Quincy Adams.

Early Years

Henry Clay was born in Hanover County, Virginia, on April 12, 1777. He was the seventh of nine children born to his parents, John and Elizabeth Clay. His father was a Baptist minister. In 1780, Henry's father became very sick. His decline was rapid; several months later, he died at the age of 38. Elizabeth, 30 years old, was left with six children to raise, and she was expecting another baby. Somehow, she had to keep the family together and care for the farm.

The War Comes to His Doorstep

To add to her **distress**, the day after she buried her husband, the war came to her doorstep. The year was 1781, and the War of Independence had been raging for six years. Four-year-old Henry was in the yard when he heard a horse galloping towards him. An American soldier was racing down the road, yelling, "Tarleton's coming! Tarleton's coming!" Henry ran to the house. That name brought fear to all the families in Hanover County. British Army General Banastre Tarleton had a reputation for

distress: Troubles

extreme cruelty. He and his troops **pillaged** the countryside, causing death and destruction.

Henry ran to alert his mother to the danger. She immediately told him to find his older brothers and get them to the house. Her husband had hired a farm manager when he got so sick he could no longer work. She sent this man into the woods to hide. Henry found his brothers, and all three boys rushed to the house. Sally and Molly, their sisters, were there already. Mrs. Clay hurriedly gave the baby to Sally and handed the little two-year-old to Molly. She instructed her girls to care for them no matter what happened.

pillaged: Violently destroyed

Tarleton's men rode into the yard. Tarleton ordered them to go to the smokehouse and take all the bacon and hams they could find. He also told them to take horses, saddles, and bridles from the barn. Some of his men came into the house to take any silver and gold they could find. Mrs. Clay told them she had none. The soldiers grabbed food, gobbling some and stuffing the rest into sacks. They then began to search the house, tearing pillows apart with their swords and chopping trunks open with an ax.

Henry Clay —The Great Peacemaker

A soldier outside hollered that he had found where Mrs. Clay had buried her **valuables**. An officer took his sword and slashed into the fresh pile of dirt in the yard. Mrs. Clay screamed for him to stop.

valuables: Items of value — dishes, silver, etc.

etched: Remembered clearly

resolving: Deciding

The pile of newly dug dirt was covering her husband's fresh grave. Seeing that she was telling the truth, they turned and raced off to pillage another farm. The awful scene was **etched** in Henry's mind. He remembered **resolving** that day that he would do whatever he could to protect his family and his country for his entire life.

Growing Up

A few months later, the British army surrendered at Yorktown, Virginia, and the War of Independence was over. Henry loved hearing the stories his mother told the children of the part Virginia had played in winning freedom. George Washington, Thomas Jefferson, and Patrick Henry were all from Virginia. Patrick Henry, famous for his speech, "Give me liberty or give me death," had grown up on a farm just a few miles from the Clay's farmhouse.

74 Famous American Statesmen

Henry attended a log school as a boy and was a fast learner. He only went to school for three years, then continued to study at home. Henry had to do many chores on the family farm. In his spare time, he went to the woods and practiced making speeches like Patrick Henry had done.

When Henry was still young, his mother remarried. The family moved to Kentucky when Henry was 14. He begged to be able to stay in Richmond and find a job to support himself. He found employment in a general store. At the same time, he applied for a position at the Virginia Court of Chancery. The court promised him a job as a **clerk** as soon as there was an opening. When he turned 15, that job became available.

Henry Clay — Clerk

The judge of the court was Mr. George Wythe, who had been one of the signers of the Declaration of Independence. Judge Wythe was impressed with Henry's neat, orderly work. The judge was an old man now, and his hand shook when he wrote. He wanted to write a book about his many law cases. He asked Henry to do the writing while he **dictated** to him what he wanted to say. Henry was thrilled! He was now secretary to the famous Judge Wythe!

> **clerk:** An administrative position
>
> **dictated:** Read aloud

Henry did neat work, but he had not learned punctuation in his three years of schooling. Judge Wythe gave him a book to learn grammar and punctuation, and Henry studied every night. When the judge wanted to use some Greek words in his book, Henry studied the Greek alphabet. Judge Wythe encouraged the boy to read whenever he had the chance. He made his **vast** library available to Henry.

Becoming a Lawyer

Henry worked with the judge for three years until the book was completed. Henry told the judge that his dream was to become a lawyer. Judge Wythe arranged for Henry to study law under Robert Brooke, who had been governor of Virginia. Brooke was very skilled in the courtroom. Henry passed the law exam when he was 20 years old. He then felt it was time to leave Virginia for Kentucky, where his family was living. His mother was delighted to see him, as were his brothers and sisters. It felt good to be back with his family. Henry set up his law practice in Lexington, Kentucky. He had a skill for capturing the rapt attention of juries and he won many cases. In Lexington, he met and soon married Lucretia Hart. They named their first son after his **mentor**, Judge Wythe.

vast: Extensive

mentor: Teacher and advisor

Legislature

The people of Kentucky elected Henry to the state legislature when he was 26 years old. He was known and admired for his passionate speeches. Henry was elected to the U.S. Senate for the first time in 1806. Thomas Jefferson was the president at the time. Henry Clay set off for Washington. The road was rough, full of holes, and scattered with rocks, which made travel difficult. When he arrived, the senators were discussing whether money should be appropriated for building bridges and roads. Henry jumped to his feet. He gave such a convincing speech that the other senators were surprised. He was the youngest one there. When his term was up, he was elected for another term. When he was 34, the state of Kentucky elected him to the House of Representatives. Clay's reputation **preceded** him. He was elected Speaker of the House on his first day in office. Never had the House elected a newcomer to be speaker.

War of 1812

Great Britain was making trouble. They began seizing American sailors and making them work on British ships. Clay expressed his opinion that America was being **scorned** by other countries for allowing such abuse to occur. He, along with President Madison, felt the United States had no choice but to declare war against Britain. The war lasted about two

preceded: Went before

scorned: Looked down upon

Henry Clay —The Great Peacemaker 77

years. When it ended, Madison chose Henry Clay to help negotiate a peace treaty. Clay sailed off for Great Britain and successfully completed his assignment.

When Henry returned, he was again elected Speaker of the House. He worked to get highways and canals built. When asked why, he responded, "To bind and connect us together."[33] Clay could **foresee** the day when the country would span the continent to the Pacific Ocean. He also worked to convince the other members of Congress that Americans needed to produce their own goods and not rely on foreign countries to provide for their needs. He wanted to prepare for the day when America would have a population of one hundred million. The other representatives were astonished, as the population then was less than 10 million. The House kept electing Clay as Speaker. His visions for America began to come true.

foresee: See beforehand

Peacemaker

The North and South began arguing over slavery. The issue was whether to let Missouri become a state and, if so, should it allow slavery? Clay suggested a compromise. This meant that each side must give up some of their demands in **deference** to the other side. Clay told them that the writers of the Constitution had done just that, and family members often do the same thing.

deference: Respect

He made a **compelling** speech. People crowded into the House to listen to him. The balcony filled up with ladies who wanted to hear his speech, which lasted for hours. He said, "Let me say to the North and to the South what a husband and wife say to each other. Both of us have faults. Neither is perfect. Let us live in peace."[34] Ladies jumped to their feet crying, "God bless you."

Clay appealed to each representative as an individual; he also gave speeches to the whole body. He worked nonstop day and night, pleading for a peaceful agreement. Finally, the House voted in favor of his plan. Missouri became a state that allowed slavery, but Maine became a state that did not allow it. Clay became known as The Great Peacemaker. John Quincy Adams was now president. He appointed Clay to be in his **Cabinet**. Henry Clay was no longer Speaker of the House. He was now Secretary of State. Clay dreamed of a great America. He sent delegates to a meeting in Panama to discuss building a canal to unite the Pacific and Atlantic Oceans, making passage open to all ships of the world. Almost 100 years later, this dream became a reality.

compelling: Convincing

Cabinet: The presidential advisory body

Henry Clay —The Great Peacemaker

Home Again

When Clay finished his term, he and Lucretia returned to Kentucky. They had a large farm with a spacious brick house. They named it Ashland because hundreds of ash trees grew there. Here they raised their children. There had been six girls and five boys, but sadly five of their daughters had died. Their oldest son was very sickly and had to spend his life in a hospital. The loss of the children was something Clay found hard to bear. He still had James and John at home, though. He built them a mile-long racetrack for their horses. They shared his love for horses. Some of their racehorses became famous. One grew up to win the English Derby. Lucretia managed the cows in their dairy, and sold their butter and cream to a hotel in Lexington. They had a flock of sheep for making wool for clothing, and even owned a herd of eight buffalo, the only herd left in Kentucky.

The Country Needs Him

One day, a letter arrived from Daniel Webster, a famous senator. "We need your arm in the fight," he wrote.[35] He wanted Clay to run for Senate. Clay had been home for only two years, but his country needed him. Kentucky again elected him senator. Off he went, back to Congress. Senator Clay and President Andrew Jackson disagreed on what was best for the country. Jackson had imposed a tax on cloth coming from England. Jackson's reason was to get people to buy American cloth instead. However, the North was charging more for cloth than England had charged.

The North could manufacture cloth in their big factories, but the South did not have factories. The people of South Carolina wanted to separate from the Union. Again, Senator Clay came up with a plan — a compromise. It had worked before, and it would work again. People crowded around to hear his speech in the Senate: "Heal the wounds of our country. We want no trouble in our family. Vote for this bill."[36] Finally, the Compromise Bill passed, and again, Clay held the reputation as the Great Peacemaker.

Clay's supporters wanted him to run for president. While preparing to make a speech, one of his friends warned him not to say anything that might hurt his chances of winning. Clay responded, "I had rather be right than be President."[37] The race ended up being a close one. Clay lost to Democrat James K. Polk. Some of his faithful supporters gathered on his front lawn to give him honor. Some of the old soldiers were weeping. Clay, however, took the defeat well.

Compromise Again

Clay went home to his farm and practiced law again. When he was very old, the state of Kentucky called on him again to settle a quarrel between the states. This time, California was requesting statehood. Again, the same old argument over the right to allow slavery was the issue. Clay drew up a compromise to present to the Senate. It was a cold February day in 1850. Clay had to stop to cough as he climbed the stairs to the Senate building.

Henry Clay —The Great Peacemaker

He was not feeling very well, but his country was in danger of dividing again. People crammed into the Senate room and spilled out into the streets to hear him. Clay was now the oldest senator, 73 years old. No other senator had been around during the War of Independence. Clay had never forgotten Tarleton's men thrusting the sword into his father's grave. Suddenly, he got a burst of energy. He spoke passionately: "We are one family. I will try to keep us together as one family."[38] His speech lasted for three whole hours. One man said that Patrick Henry was the only other man who could hold an audience spellbound like that.

Some people accused Henry Clay of siding with the North. Others accused him of siding with the South. He responded, "I know no South, no North, no East, no West . . . My allegiance is to this American Union! This Union is my country. The 30 states are my country."[39] It took seven long months, but the Compromise Bill of 1850 finally passed. Henry Clay contracted tuberculosis two years later and died, still working as senator from Kentucky. Clay's commitment to his country inspired many other **statesmen** to stand for the principles they believed in. It was said, "Henry Clay helped to save his country until it was strong enough to save itself."[40]

statesmen: Skilled and respected political leaders

7

Francis Scott Key –
The Star-Spangled Banner

August 1, 1779 – January 11, 1843

Who Was Francis Scott Key?

Statesman, poet, lawyer, district attorney, and author of the national anthem, Francis Scott Key wanted to be useful to his country. He achieved that goal.

Early Years

Francis Scott Key was born on August 1, 1779, in Frederick County, Maryland. His family owned a large farm that was called *Terra Rubra*, named for the red dirt that covered their land. Francis and his sister Anne loved to roam the woods and fields. They had cows, horses, and a sheepdog to guard their sheep. The dog was named "General" after General Washington. Francis' father, a lawyer and a judge, had fought alongside General George Washington during the War of Independence. He returned to his career when the war ended, traveling about holding court. The family loved books and music and had an **extensive** library. Mrs. Key read to the children each night. They sang hymns together as well. In later years, Francis, known as Frank, said he could not remember a time when his mother did not have her Bible nearby. She taught her

extensive: Large

children to read and write using the Bible as their textbook. They learned early that the Bible was the guidebook for their lives.

Grandmother Key

Grandmother Key lived in Annapolis, Maryland. The children loved to visit Grandmother Key. As a young girl, her parents had owned slaves. One night, her father's house caught on fire. Two of their slaves were trapped in the house. Grandmother Key had rushed in and saved them. The fire and smoke blinded her eyes, and she never saw again, but she never regretted saving those lives.

Frank would read the Bible to Grandmother whenever he visited. She took him to church, and they said prayers together. Frank learned to speak clearly with great expression while keeping quiet and calm at the same time. Years later, people asked him his secret of being able to speak in public and make others understand what he said. He **attributed** his skill to communicating with his blind grandmother.

attributed: Gave credit to

Off to School

Frank went to grammar school in Annapolis, Maryland. He hated to leave Terra Rubra and always went home during the summer months. When he was 12, he came home to hear exciting news: George Washington was to visit Terra Rubra on his way to the nation's capital, which was in Philadelphia. George Washington was his hero. He had listened often to his father tell of marching 520 miles to Boston to join Washington's army during the Revolution. His father had been there with Washington and Lafayette at Yorktown, too.

Neighbors from miles around came that day. Men who had been soldiers showed up in their uniforms. People carried flags, and all were excited to see President Washington. When his father introduced Francis to the great leader, the president said, "You have a proud name. See that you live up to it."[41] Washington talked with Frank's father and the old soldiers about the war. When he left, Frank told Anne he was proud of his family, his country, and his president. He said, "One day, I will try to make them proud of me."[42]

College

Frank went to college at St. John's after he completed grammar school. He was well-liked by his fellow students. He and his friend John Shaw enjoyed writing poems and sharing them with each other. Frank seemed to be able to compose a poem for any situation.

Frank often saw his Uncle Philip Barton Key, a **prominent** lawyer in Maryland. He began reading Uncle Philip's many law books and discussed what he learned with his uncle. Frank graduated with honors when he was 17 and went home for the summer. When he went back to Annapolis that fall, it was to study law under Judge Jeremiah Chase. Another young man, Roger Taney, was one of Chase's students and the two became fast friends.

prominent: Important

Frank now lived with his uncle in Annapolis. Here he met Mary Taylor Lloyd, the daughter of a wealthy Maryland family. Frank playfully gave her the nickname Polly. He began writing her poems. When he asked if she liked them, she **coyly** answered that they made fine curling paper for her hair each night. He told his sister Anne that he had three goals: to marry Polly, to become a good lawyer, and to see Thomas Jefferson become president. In 1800, Frank opened up his law practice in Frederick, Maryland. In 1801, Thomas Jefferson became president. The following year, Frank married Polly. Within three years, his three goals had been met.

coyly: With cute or casual playfulness

Francis Scott Key—The Star-Spangled Banner

Lawyer Key

Uncle Philip had moved to Washington, D.C., and invited Francis to join him in his law practice. Frank accepted. He and Polly bought a house in Georgetown near Washington. They gave parties and dinners and made many friends. It wasn't long before Uncle Philip was elected to Congress and turned his entire practice over to Francis.

Francis' first famous case was his defense of Aaron Burr, who was found taking guns and men to the southwest to possibly lead a rebellion against the U.S. government. All the men involved were charged with **treason**. No lawyer wanted to take the case. Francis felt everyone should have a fair trial and decided he would represent them. The case was heard before the United States Supreme Court. Burr and his codefendants were found not guilty. Francis impressed everyone in the courtroom. People said he was a born speaker. One friend said, "His face seemed to shed sparkling beams upon his words as they fell from his lips."[43]

Key had many **affluent** clients, but he also spent much time defending poor people. He never charged old soldiers who had fought in the War of Independence. He also defended African American slaves who were trying to gain their freedom. Virginia Congressman John Randolph, a friend of Francis Key, once asked him why he was always helping those who could not pay. Key answered, "I do good only for the joy of seeing good done."[44]

treason: The crime of betraying one's country

affluent: Wealthy

Francis always tried to take time to play with his children. Friends would remark that the family always seemed to have a good time. Key was also quite involved in working for the community. He helped to establish the first public school in Washington. Francis was very involved in church and taught Sunday school. He consistently gave money to help the church as well as the poor.

Washington Is Burning

In the early 1800s, England was in a war with France. To keep American ships from taking goods to France, English sea captains captured American sailors. They then forced them to serve on English ships. This had to be stopped; ultimately, Congress declared war on England. The War of 1812 began. Key joined the army. In August 1814, the British began their attack on Washington. On August 24, they burned the President's Mansion, the Capitol building, and the Library of Congress.

A few days later, Polly's brother informed Key that the British had captured Dr. William Beanes, the faithful doctor who had treated soldiers during the War of Independence. Some **rowdy** English soldiers had started a fight on his property, and Dr. Beanes had reported them to the authorities. They were jailed overnight. The British were angry and took the doctor prisoner. He was being held on a British ship in Baltimore harbor.

Francis said he must get Dr. Beanes freed. President James Madison gave Key permission to seek Dr. Beanes' release, and sent a government agent, Colonel Skinner, to accompany him. Key and Skinner flew a white flag of peace as they reached the English **flagship**, the *Tonnant*. Francis used his persuasive skills as he begged for the old doctor's release. He told how the doctor had recently treated English soldiers wounded in battle. At last, the English agreed to let him go, but said they must wait until after the attack they were planning on Fort McHenry in Baltimore.

The Flag Was Still There

Fort McHenry, a star-shaped brick outpost, guarded the entrance to the harbor. Major George Armistead, the commandant, ordered a

rowdy: Disorderly

flagship: A ship that carries the commanding admiral

Famous American Statesmen

huge "fair weather" flag to fly over the fort. It was 42 feet wide by 30 feet high, called the "Great Garrison Flag." Mary Pickersgill, a local seamstress, was asked to make the giant flag. She and her 14-year-old daughter worked tirelessly. When it was finished, it was the largest flag ever flown for a battle. On September 13, the British ships moved into formation to attack the fort by sea. Key, Colonel Skinner, and Dr. Beanes were under guard but were able to watch the battle from the ship. Francis paced the deck, feeling completely helpless. Then he remembered what Grandmother Key had always told him: "Remember Francis, you can always pray, even by yourself. That is always something you can do."[45] Francis began to pray in earnest.

The Bombardment of Fort McHenry

Soon the bombardment of Fort McHenry began. All day long British bombs fell on the fort. One of the stars on the giant flag was torn away. The British ships were too far away for the fort's guns to reach them. The attack **intensified** that night. **Rockets** created flashes of light as they were aimed at the fort. Then it began to rain. The British ships sailed in

intensified: Grew stronger

rockets: Bombs that propel themselves

Francis Scott Key—The Star-Spangled Banner

closer, hoping to complete their mission. Finally, they were close enough for the guns from Fort McHenry to reach them. The sky blazed with gunfire. Heavy smoke hung over the bay. Francis couldn't sleep all night. His eyes were fixed on that flag. As long as the flag stood fast, Fort McHenry had not surrendered.

Francis took out an envelope from his pocket. He began writing a few lines for a poem. More words came to him. That flag **symbolized** freedom and courage. Words kept coming, and Francis kept scribbling, checking every few minutes to see if the flag was still there. Finally, there was so much smoke that he could no longer see the flag.

> **symbolized:** Stood for

Toward morning, the gunfire suddenly stopped. All Francis could do was pray and keep scribbling as words came to him.

As dawn broke, Francis could finally see clearly. "It's there!" he cried. "The flag still waves. Baltimore is saved!"[46] Dr. Beanes strained to see. "Are you sure, Francis?" "Yes, yes! It is ours. It's our beloved red, white, and blue. May God be praised!"[47] Key later recalled thinking, "Then, in that hour of deliverance and joyful triumph, my heart spoke; and 'Does not such a country and such defenders of their country deserve a song?' was the question."[48]

The British took the three Americans ashore. That night in Baltimore, Colonel Skinner, Dr. Beanes, and Francis had supper. When the other two men headed for bed, Francis asked the innkeeper for paper, ink, and quill. Referring to the notes on the envelope, he began to write. He hummed the tune of an old song, "To Acaecreon of Heaven." Key's first verse posed the question he had prayed all night. "Oh say, does that star-spangled banner yet wave, O'er the land of the free and home of the brave?" The last verse provides the answer, "And the star-spangled banner in triumph shall wave O'er the land of the free and the home of the brave."

The next morning, Francis showed his poem to Judge Nicholson, his brother-in-law. He had been the second in command of Fort McHenry while it was under attack. He excitedly told Francis it must be printed at once and rushed to the office of the *Baltimore American*, the city's newspaper. The owner was gone, fighting with the army, but 14-year-old Samuel Sands was watching over the shop. Sands printed the poem, and the papers were quickly passed out to the public. People began singing and it was published in papers all over the country. It later was given the title of *The Star-Spangled Banner*.

Francis Scott Key—The Star-Spangled Banner

Home Again

Francis was overjoyed to head back home to his family. His fame as a lawyer spread, as did his fame for having written the song. He handled many law cases that became important in the history of American law. He got more invitations to speak than he was able to handle. People treated him as a hero, but he said the real heroes were those who had defended their country.

When President Andrew Jackson was elected president, he appointed Francis Scott Key to be the United States Attorney General for the District of Columbia. President Jackson chose Key to help settle a dispute in Alabama with land given to the Creek Native Americans. He told Key, "If anyone can bring peace, you can."[49] Six weeks later, Key returned home. Peace had been achieved.

Francis and Polly had 11 children in all, although 3 died. During those times of loss, Key drew strength from the Lord and the Bible.

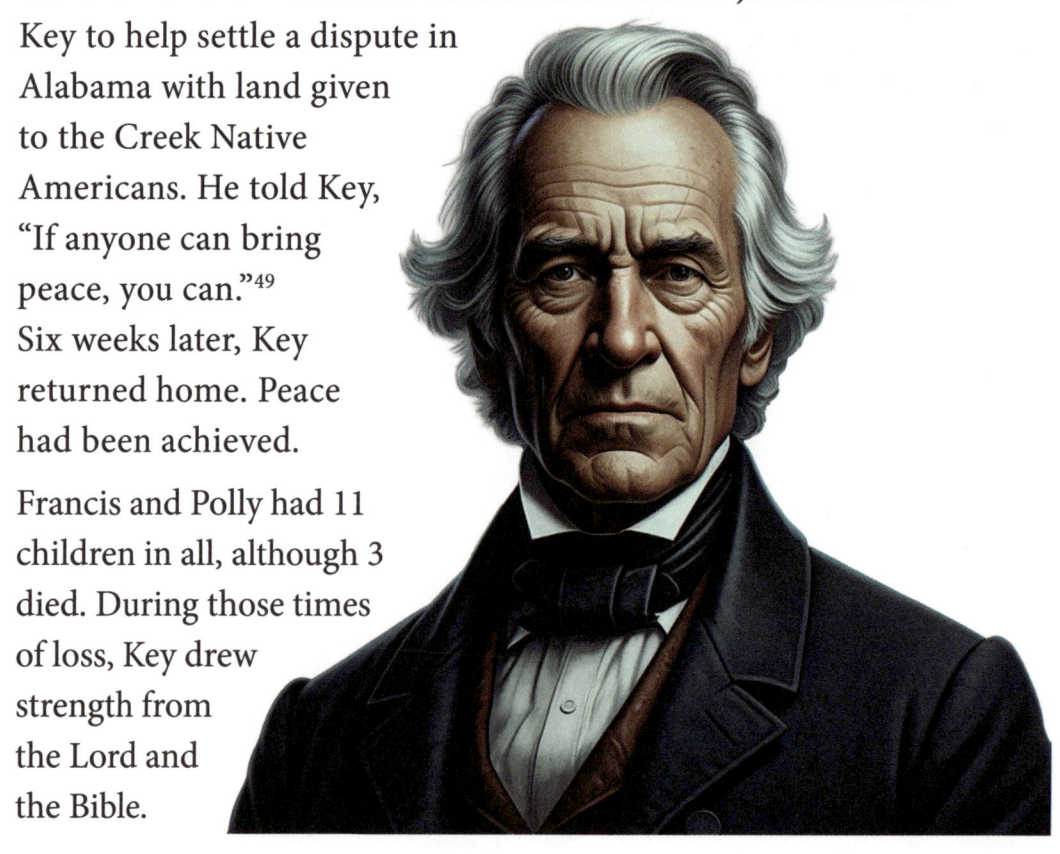

Famous American Statesmen

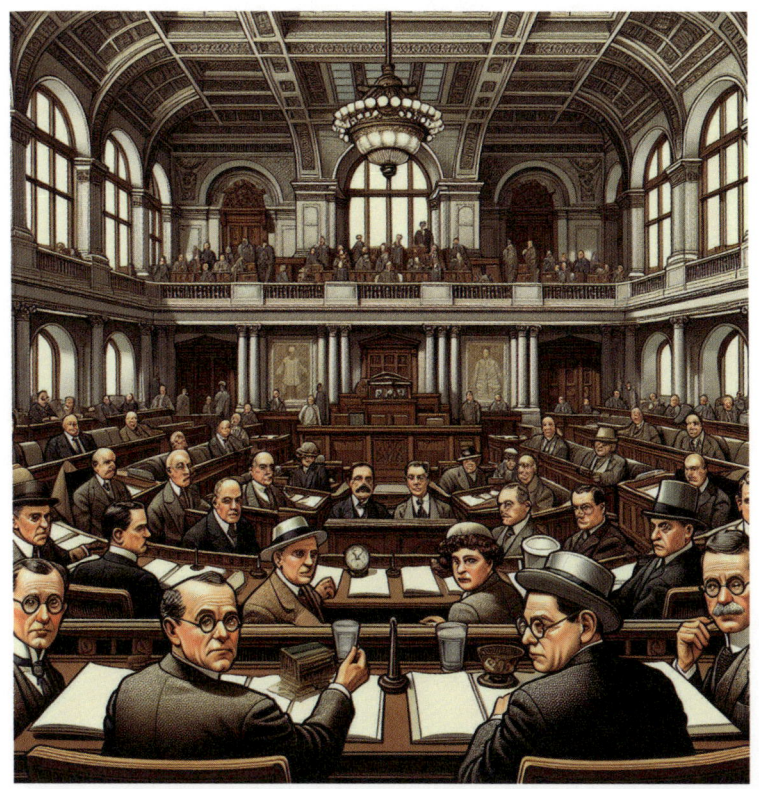

As Key grew older, he took fewer law cases but devoted more time to helping the community. He worked to try to find an answer to the problem of slavery and influenced many others to help. He also found ways to help freed slaves learn to read and earn money.

In early 1843, he was called to Baltimore on business. He had a very bad cold when he left. He stayed with his daughter Elizabeth when he arrived in Baltimore, and quickly grew very ill. Just before he went to bed, he told Elizabeth, "Remember, the money in the bag is for the poor."[50] That night he died peacefully in his sleep.

In 1931, Congress declared "The Star-Spangled Banner" to be our country's official National Anthem. As a remembrance of Francis Scott Key and a tribute to our nation, let us always remember the words of the last verse of the beloved national anthem:

O! Thus be it ever when free men shall stand

Between their lov'd home and the war's desolation!

Blest with vict'ry and peace, may the heav'n rescued land

Praise the Power that hath made and preserv'd us a nation!

Then conquer we must, when our cause it is just;

And this be our motto — "In God is our trust,"

And the star-spangled banner in triumph shall wave

O'er the land of the free and the home of the brave.

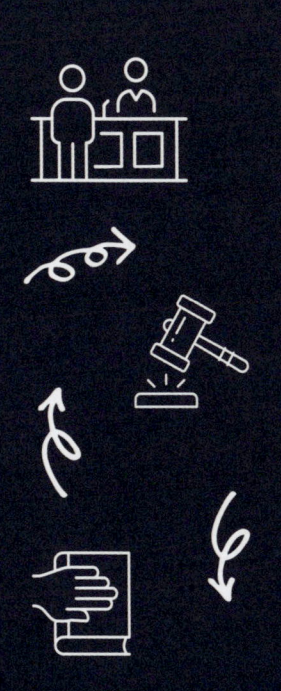

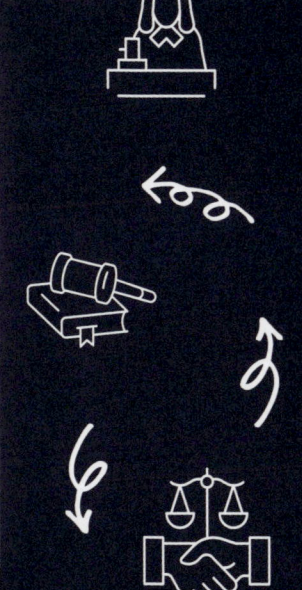

8

Daniel Webster –

Defender of the Constitution

January 18, 1782 – October 24, 1852

Who Was Daniel Webster?

Daniel Webster is known as the greatest **orator** in the history of the United States Senate. He believed "that to become a great orator, one must study the Word of God and read the Bible aloud."[51]

Early Years

Daniel Webster was born January 18, 1782, in Salisbury, New Hampshire, to Ebenezer and Abigail Webster. His father, a judge, had been a captain in the War of Independence. Daniel was thrilled to sit on his father's lap and hear stories of his experiences in the war. His father was his hero. Daniel could repeat his father's stories word for word. Captain Webster had **mustered** a troop of 200 men from their hometown immediately after hearing about the Battles of Lexington and Concord. He had been present when Washington heard of the **treachery** of Benedict Arnold. The great Washington had asked Daniel's father to be his bodyguard that night. He had said, "Captain Webster, I believe I can trust you."[52] Daniel hoped that one day he, too, would be trusted to do some brave deed for his country.

Daniel had nine siblings. He was often sickly as a boy, but Daniel had a strong mind. He could read the Bible by the time he was five

orator: Skilled speaker

mustered: Gathered

treachery: Betrayal

years old. He never forgot what he read. As Daniel grew, his job was to run the family's sawmill, which gave him time to read. He would set a log on the mill, start the blade, and sit down to enjoy a book. Daniel's favorite book to read was the Bible, but he read whatever he could get his hands on. Men who came to the mill begged him to read to them from the Bible. Daniel used dramatic expression and emphasis that made the Bible come alive when he read.

Daniel was always the brightest boy in school. A schoolmaster would come periodically to teach neighborhood children. One day, he announced to the children that they would have a contest to see who could memorize the most Bible verses in the eight weeks. The teacher had each child come to the front of the class to quote their verses. One girl quoted 52 verses with no mistakes. Then Daniel had his turn. He started with Psalm 1, then Psalm 2, 3, 4, 5, 6. He was definitely in the lead, but he did not stop: Psalm 7, 8, 9, 10. He was at 120 verses when the schoolmaster made him stop. He declared him the winner. Daniel's reward was a brand-new jackknife, that would have been a basic folding pocketknife.

His Own Copy of the Constitution

When a store opened in Salisbury, Daniel saw a handkerchief on which was printed the Constitution of the United States. The edges were decorated with military flags and emblems. Daniel had never seen a copy of the Constitution until then, and he had to have that handkerchief. He purchased it, showed it to everyone, and carried it wherever he went. He never let it go long enough even to have it washed. He read it over again and again, memorizing the words and learning ideas that influenced him his entire life.

More Education

Daniel's father arranged for him to be tutored by Dr. Samuel Wood, a minister from a nearby village who helped prepare Daniel for college. Dr. Wood began teaching him Latin, mathematics, geography, Greek, and history. He made his extensive library available to Daniel as well. Whatever Daniel read, he would then discuss with Dr. Wood during the evening meal. When Daniel could read the four gospels in Greek, Dr. Wood told him he was prepared to enter Dartmouth College.

Daniel was only 15 years old when he began studying at Dartmouth. He loved college. He had an advantage over most other students. When he thoroughly understood information he was reading, he remembered it and could often quote it word for word. He and his fellow students had **stimulating** discussions about world events.

Daniel had a growing enthusiasm for history and read all he could. He read speeches by famous men and read about debates taking place in Congress. To help pay for his education, he took a job for the *Dartmouth Gazette*, a small weekly newspaper. He got the position of **superintendent** of publications. He was asked to present the Fourth of July oration for the city of Hanover at a special service **commemorating** the 24th anniversary of the signing of the Declaration of Independence. No student had ever received such an honor. Daniel was excited to tell about the late President Washington's unequaled contribution to the cause of freedom. Daniel studied and wrote out his speech, word for word. He memorized it and practiced speaking it out in the woods and fields. It was worth all his efforts; the audience sat **spellbound** as he spoke.

stimulating: Enjoyably exciting or interesting

superintendent: Manager

commemorating: Remembering and honoring

spellbound: Fascinated

The Study of Law

Daniel served as a clerk under the skilled lawyer Christopher Gore. President Washington had placed Gore in the office of District Attorney for Massachusetts. Mr. Gore agreed to let Daniel study law books in his office. He also encouraged him to attend the meetings of the Massachusetts Supreme Court and United States District Court. He made his personal library available to Daniel as well. Daniel had struggled to make ends meet and had even made time to work as a teacher to help **augment** his family's finances. His father was able to secure a good job for him as Clerk of Court in Hillsboro. Daniel was tempted to take it but asked the advice of Mr. Gore. Mr. Gore advised him, "You can be more than a clerk. You can be an actor on the stage of life rather than a recorder of other men's actions. Go on, and finish your studies; you are poor enough, but there are greater evils than poverty. Live on no man's favor. What bread you eat, let it be the bread of independence."[53] This advice confirmed for Daniel what he had **contemplated** since his college days. The "God who controlled the affairs of men as well as nations had something specific for him to do."[54] He would persevere! In two months, he completed his education and was able to practice law on his own.

> **augment:** Add to
>
> **contemplated:** Thought about

102   Famous American Statesmen

Daniel Webster — Lawyer

Daniel opened his practice in Boscawen, New Hampshire, where he could be close enough to help care for his aging parents. He also began attending his old church again and resolved to be regular in attendance. The first Sunday back, he met Miss Grace Fletcher, a minister's daughter who was teaching school. He discovered she had read many of the same books he had, and they enjoyed discussing ideas together.

Daniel also dedicated himself to a thorough study of God's Word he had so **aptly** memorized as a child. He wanted to communicate its truth to others. His goal was to be able to defend the providence of God, the divinity of Christ, and the authority of the Scriptures logically from the Word. Grace, too, had become a Christian at an early age and wanted to be sure the man she married would center his life in the person of Christ. Her first concern was how to please her Maker. Daniel met those qualifications, and the couple was married on June 24, 1808. Daniel bought a house for them in Portsmouth, near his law practice.

aptly: Skillfully

Daniel Webster —Defender of the Constitution

War of 1812

Daniel used his gift of oratory to influence others. He always supported the Constitution of the United States. Three weeks after Congress declared war on Great Britain, he delivered a compelling speech before the Portsmouth chapter of the **Washington Benevolent Society**. The British were taking American men off their ships and forcing them to work for the British navy. Webster believed that these abuses occurring on the sea should be fought on the sea and not on the land. He strongly felt the president should abandon any thought of invading Canada, being responsible for bringing the conflict to an "early and honorable close."[55]

> **Washington Benevolent Society:** A charitable organization that supported the Federalist Party

Copies of his speech were printed and distributed throughout New Hampshire. Daniel was elected as a delegate for the people of Portsmouth. There he delivered a 90-minute speech in protest of the war and held the listeners spellbound. In November of 1812, the people elected Webster to the House of Representatives. Daniel was 31 years old at the time. His strong opposition to the war brought him to the attention of politicians Henry Clay and John Calhoun. They recognized that he was an opponent, but equal to themselves in oratory skills.

Influencing Others

Webster delivered many speeches while in the House that helped to change the course of the nation over the next 40 years. In 1814, he opposed a bill that would force men to be drafted into the army. He argued that it was the right of each state to raise its own militia. After the death of his daughter, Gracie, in 1816, Daniel moved back to Boston to his law practice. He wanted to spend more time with his other children. He bought a large house on Beacon Street, and he and the family did much entertaining. Once they even had the beloved Marquis de Lafayette as a guest. Each evening Daniel gathered his children and read to them. Grace knitted as she listened. He would be the first to arise each morning and wake his family by singing hymns at the top of his voice. His children remembered these days as some of the best of their growing-up years.

Daniel's work as a lawyer sometimes led him to argue before the Supreme Court of the United States. One of his most famous presentations was his defense of his old **alma mater**, Dartmouth College. He gave a rousing speech defending its right to remain a private institution and retain its own policies.

> **alma mater:** The school from which one graduates

He argued that not doing so was in opposition to Article I, Section 10 of the Constitution of the United States, the document he had so faithfully memorized from the handkerchief he purchased as a boy. Daniel Webster won his greatest case before the Supreme Court by upholding the Constitution.

Two years later, Daniel Webster gave another famous speech in Plymouth, Massachusetts, that was printed and distributed. School children memorized parts of it for recitation. He delivered the speech on December 22, 1820, in honor of the Pilgrims who had landed there 200 years earlier. Twelve hundred people squeezed into First Church of Plymouth to hear him speak. One man wrote that he "was never so excited by public speaking before in his life."[56] Webster told of the Pilgrim fathers who came to this land to spread the good news of the gospel of Christ. He gave glory to God for the blessings this country had experienced. Thousands of people agreed it was the most stirring speech ever given in the history of the country.

Daniel Webster continued to work for his country throughout his life. In addition to serving in the United States Congress, he served as U.S. Secretary of State under three presidents: William Henry Harrison, John Tyler, and Millard Fillmore. As one of the most prominent lawyers of the 19th century, Webster argued more than 200 cases before the United States Supreme Court during his lifetime.

Final Days

Late in July 1852, Daniel Webster left Washington, D.C. for the last time. He returned to his home in Marshfield, Massachusetts. He found a large crowd of neighbors waiting to greet him at the station. He was pleased and invited them to his home where he delivered his last speech. He had not been feeling well. For the next three months, he battled an illness, now thought to be liver disease. He was confined to bed in October. He called his only surviving child, Daniel Fletcher, and some close friends to his bedside. He talked to them about God and how he had trusted in Him from his childhood and assured all that he would be spending eternity in heaven. Early the next morning, October 24, 1852, Daniel Webster died.

As a dear friend testified, "He loved and read the Bible as it ought to be loved and read. He read it aloud to his family every Sunday morning.... He never made a journey without carrying a copy with him and I testify that I never listened to the story of the Savior ... when it sounded so superbly eloquent as when coming from his lips."[57] The entire nation mourned for the man who had lived his whole life as a champion of the Constitution of the United States.

9

Sam Houston –

Hero of Texas

March 2, 1793 – July 26, 1863

Who Was Sam Houston?

Sam Houston was an American general and statesman. He was a leader in the Texas Revolution. He served as the first and the third president of the Republic of Texas. He was instrumental in helping Texas become a state and was elected as one of the first two U.S. senators from Texas.

Boyhood Days

Sam Houston was born on March 2, 1793, in Rockbridge County, Virginia. His father, Samuel, was a major general in the U.S. Army and served in the local militia as well. He had fought in the War of Independence to help win our country's freedom from Great Britain. Sam was proud of his father and wanted to be a general, too. Because his father was away much of the time, his wife, Elizabeth, ran the family farm with the help of her children. They all worked hard, but the family was poor. Sam was schooled most of the time at home by his mother. His father had taught him to read out of *The Manual of Arms*. It was the book used to train soldiers. His father told him he was the best soldier of his size in Virginia. Sam loved reading, and he loved exploring the woods and fields around the farm.

Sam had his own "army" composed of his younger brother Willy and some friends. During the brief time he did attend the log schoolhouse, he drilled his "army" before they headed off for school. He, of course, was their captain. They were often late for school. Sam would let the teacher know it was his fault and then lead his "army" into the school building.

Life Changes

Sam's father died suddenly in 1807 when Sam was 14. His father had bought land in Tennessee and had been planning to move the family there. So the family headed for Tennessee, as General Houston would have wanted. Sam helped his brothers cut down trees to build a log cabin. They planted crops and tended them. Sam hated farming. He tried working in the general store but didn't like that any better. Sam became bored. He wanted some adventure.

Finally, Sam left home and joined a tribe of peaceful Cherokees. Chief Oolooteka taught him many things, such as how to use a bow and arrow. The chief liked Sam, called him his son, and gave him the name Co-lon-neh, which means The Raven. To the Cherokees, a raven was their good luck bird. Giving this name to Sam showed that they respected him greatly. The Indian boys asked Sam to race, and he won every time.

Sam lived with the Cherokees for three years. Sam dressed in Cherokee clothes and learned their language and customs. He learned to move quietly through the woods like the Cherokee boys. He went to his brother's store occasionally with deerskins to exchange for goods to give to the Cherokee he considered his brothers. Several times, his deerskins didn't cover the cost of the goods he took, so he promised to get more skins. Eventually, he owed $100. He told the chief he must go to his old home for a while to pay off his debts.

U.S. Army

Shortly after Sam arrived home, the town held a spelling bee. He participated, and at first, people thought he wouldn't be able to compete. However, Sam was still an avid reader and a good speller. He surprised everyone by winning the spelling bee. Someone said, "You should be a teacher." *That's an idea*, he thought. He opened a small school, and pupils flocked to it. Soon, he had his debts paid off. He planned to go back to the Cherokee village, but about this time, the War of 1812 started. Sam joined the army to help defend his country. His mother cried when he left, but she gave him his father's musket: "Never disgrace it, Sam. Never turn your back to save your life."[58] Sam promised, and off he went. An officer soon noticed Sam's skills. After all, Sam had learned to read from *The Manual of Arms* and knew it by heart.

The First Battle

By the spring of 1814, he was **Ensign** Houston, fighting under General Andrew Jackson. The Creek tribe, working with the British, had attacked a fort, killing every man, woman, and child. Jackson led his men to attack the Creeks. Sam was the first man to charge over a wall after the warriors. He got an arrow in his left leg above his knee. He asked a fellow soldier to pull it out. The soldier jerked, and blood spattered everywhere. Sam's buddies tied the wound for him and continued the attack. Sam tried to follow but was too dizzy, so he lay there for a couple of hours.

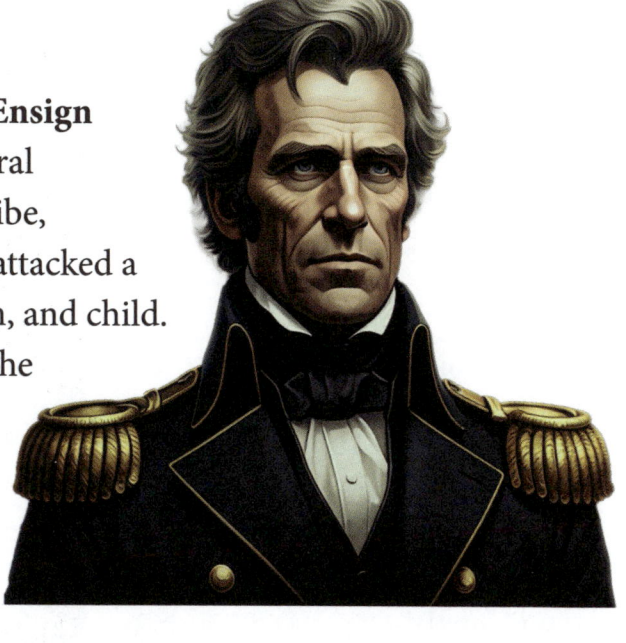

The enemy was losing, but those warriors who were still able to fight were hiding in a fairly **impenetrable** shelter. Later that afternoon, Jackson asked for volunteers to charge, acknowledging that it was a dangerous mission. Sam remembered his mother telling him, "Remember that while the door to my cabin is open to brave men, it is eternally shut against cowards."[59]

Sam volunteered and hobbled painfully toward the battle. Though there were many dead warriors, Sam knew how the Creeks thought. He knew fighting would continue until every warrior was dead. Sam borrowed a musket and started forward. He fired into one of the openings in their shelter. Almost as soon as he fired, he was hit by two bullets, one in his shoulder and one in his

Ensign: Commissioned officer

impenetrable: Hard to get to

Sam Houston — Hero of Texas

arm. Despite Sam's terrible condition, he helped capture the stronghold and set it on fire. He had done his duty; then he fell, unconscious.

He awoke to hear someone ask the doctor if he had gotten the bullets out. The doctor answered, "One. There is no use removing the other. He won't last the night. He's lost too much blood."[60] The next morning, Sam was still alive. He was put on a stretcher and dragged to Fort Williams where he was left with no medical care. When the troops returned to the fort, they **rigged** a **horse litter** and brought Sam home to his mother. It was two months since he'd been injured. It took weeks before he got well. He got a letter from Jackson saying he'd been promoted to lieutenant for his bravery. The war ended in 1815, shortly after Sam returned to his regiment.

rigged: Quickly threw together

horse litter: Bed pulled between two horses

Help for the Cherokees

Sometime later, one of his Cherokee "brothers" came to see him. The warrior explained that the U.S. government had promised the Cherokees good lands in Arkansas territory in exchange for land in Tennessee. The land, however, had not been as good as the land they had given up. They were promised that a government agent would see to any needs they had. The government also pledged money to the Cherokees as part of the exchange agreement. The Cherokees needed money for cattle, tools, supplies, and crops. The government agent cheated them.

The Cherokee brother begged Sam to apply for the job as a government agent for the Cherokee nation. He told Sam that he and his brother had been scouts for the American army in the battle where Sam was wounded. They heard what General Jackson said about Sam Houston. Sam wanted to know what Jackson had said. The Cherokee warrior quoted Jackson: "'This boy will go far, if he lives, and will do great things for his people.' We are your people, Sam. Will you try to get the appointment as agent?"[61] He told Sam he felt sure that General Jackson would help him get it. That night, Sam decided he should go to the aid of his friends, the Cherokees. The next day, he rode his horse to Jackson's home, The Hermitage, and explained the problem. Jackson wrote a letter to Washington, recommending Sam for the job.

Sam Houston — Hero of Texas

Other Jobs for Sam

It took a long time to hear back from Washington, however. In the meantime, Sam ran for the office of prosecuting attorney of the Nashville district, and won easily. He was very popular as a man and as a war hero, and so he was elected major general in the Tennessee militia after that. In 1825, the people of Tennessee chose him as their congressman. In 1827, he ran for governor of Tennessee and won.

After his term as governor was up, Sam wanted to return to visit his Cherokee brothers. He found that they had been forced to move again. He was welcomed warmly by his "father" Oolooteka. Houston went to visit all his old friends, embracing them. The Cherokees held a feast in his honor. The men made speeches. When it was Sam's turn he told them, "The government's promises were not kept.... Money was not paid.... You were promised vast hunting lands to the west. But those lands are roamed by … the plains Indians who dislike the Cherokees as much as they dislike the white man.... The plains Indians kill you. The white man cheats you. Whatever strength there is in The Raven's arm, whatever courage there is in his heart is yours to command. The Raven has come home."[62]

Sam visited other Native American settlements, listening to their **grievances** and promising to try to help them. He was soon known as the most powerful man helping the Native Americans who had been forced to leave their lands.

A short while later, Sam contracted malaria and suffered from burning fever and chills. Oolooteka cared for him. When he recovered, he observed a Cherokee agent named Duval grossly cheating the Cherokees. Duval was supposed to have paid them in gold but did not.

> **grievances:** Complaints

As a strategy, the Cherokees officially adopted Sam Houston and made him a citizen of the Cherokee nation. As such, he headed to Washington to represent their grievances to the federal government. Oolooteka sent a letter with him saying, "Great Father, My son The Raven came to me last spring.... He has walked straight, his path is not crooked. He is leaving me now to meet his white father General Jackson.... I hope he will take him by the hand and keep him as near to the heart as I have done. He is beloved of all my people."[63]

Houston wore his Cherokee clothing when he went to see President Jackson at the White House. Sam presented his evidence, and

Sam Houston — Hero of Texas

Jackson immediately dismissed the corrupt agents. Houston defended and represented the Cherokees many more times.

Off to Texas

Trouble was brewing in Texas. President Jackson asked Sam Houston to go to Texas as his eyes and ears to find out what was happening. At that time, Texas was part of Mexico, but rulers in Mexico were **tyrants**. Sam became a Texan and opened up a law office in Nacogdoches. He told President Jackson, "I believe nine-tenths of the Texans want to rebel against Mexico. If they won their independence they would want to join the United States."[64]

> **tyrants:** Oppressive rulers

War between Texas and Mexico started in 1835. General Santa Anna, the president of Mexico, ordered all Texans to give up their guns. He declared that any man bearing arms would be shot.

How could men even hunt without their guns? How could they protect their families from hostile Native Americans? Texans called a convention. Nacogdoches sent Sam as its representative to the convention; the convention sent Sam as its representative to Native Americans in the north. His assignment was to get a commitment that they would not help the Mexicans fight the Texans. Sam got a promise from the Cherokees.

The Alamo

Sam arrived back to Texas just in time to hear that the Mexicans were attacking the **Alamo**. Colonel Travis and 150 Americans were trapped inside. The next day, Texas declared its independence from Mexico. The people elected Sam Houston as Commander-in-Chief. Sam rushed orders to three different generals to try to get help to the brave men at the Alamo. Travis was running out of ammunition. Sam jumped on his horse and, with several other men, headed for the Alamo. Four days later, before he arrived, he heard the news that Santa Anna had killed every man in the Alamo.

> **Alamo:** An old Catholic mission used as a fort

On April 21, 1836, Sam faced Santa Anna. He had only 800 men. Santa Anna had over 1,300. What Texans lacked in numbers, though, they made up with the element of surprise. The Texans started across the plain for Santa Anna's camp. Sam Houston rode back and forth in front of his men ordering them to hold their fire. The Mexicans fired. Sam's horse was shot from under him. Still he yelled, "Hold your fire!" while racing before his men. Another horse was shot out from under him. When he mounted the third horse, he yelled, "Remember the Alamo! Fire!"[65]

Sam Houston — Hero of Texas

Sam's plan worked. The Mexican forces were caught off guard. Some were asleep. Some were playing cards. The battle lasted only half an hour before the Mexicans surrendered. Santa Anna had been asleep, too. When he saw one of his finest divisions fleeing, he leaped upon a big black horse and rode away as fast as he could.

Sam rode back to his camp and suddenly became dizzy. One of his men grabbed him as he fell from his saddle. When Sam woke up a doctor was working on his leg. He told him both bones were crushed just above the ankle. Sam's first words were, "Did we get Santa Anna?" "No," he was told. He warned his men to be looking for someone dressed as a common soldier. He expected Santa Anna to disguise himself. The next day his men brought in a Mexican prisoner in an ordinary soldier's uniform. Santa Anna's fellow Mexican prisoners cried, "El Presidente!" The Texans had caught him after all. Texas was free. The war was over!

President of Texas

The doctor wanted Sam to get to New Orleans to be treated, but Sam had things he wanted to accomplish first. Finally, though, he had to get medical care. It took about a month for him to recover. The Texans elected Sam President of Texas by a huge margin. Sam was hoping Texas would be admitted to the United States right away, but at the time there were disagreements over free states and slave states. Nine years later, in 1845, Texas became the 28th state to join the United States of America. Sam was elected president of Texas for two terms, as its first and third president.

At last, Sam Houston thought he would have time to enjoy his family, but that would have to wait. He was elected as one of the first two senators from Texas in 1846. For years in this office, Sam fought to hold the Union together. Texas elected him governor in 1859, just before the onset of the Civil War. Sam, although a Southerner, made many speeches against **secession**. Nevertheless, Texas left the Union in 1861.

Sam had to do what he felt was right. He gave up the governorship and went home to the little town of Huntsville, Texas. He moved his family into an unusual house shaped like a steamboat! He had eight children, and now he had time to enjoy them. The Civil War began in April 1861. In the summer of 1863, Sam caught a cold. It

secession: The formal withdrawal of a state from the United States

Sam Houston — Hero of Texas

developed into **pneumonia**. He said he must get better because Texas would need him when the war was over. However, in July of that year, 70-year-old Sam Houston died.

The city of Houston is named for Sam Houston, the beloved hero of Texas. The San Jacinto monument marks the battleground where Sam and his small army defeated the Mexican army and gained independence for Texas.

pneumonia: Infection of the lungs

10

William Jennings Bryan – Champion of the Common Man

March 19, 1860 – July 26, 1925

Who Was William Jennings Bryan?

Everywhere Congressman Bryan spoke, crowds cheered and applauded. He was called the "Golden-Tongued Orator." He was known for fighting for the **common** people against the power of big corporations and **monopolies**. As a dedicated Christian, he defended the working class against the evils of society and government. He was perhaps best known for his stand on creation and the Bible in the "Scopes Monkey Trials."

> **common:** Working class
>
> **monopolies:** Companies with exclusive control over an industry

Boyhood Days

The Civil War started one month after Willy Bryan was born to Silas and Mariah Bryan. The family lived in Salem, Illinois. They opened their home on many evenings for friends to come and discuss politics, religion, and the war. They had friends from both the North and the South. Each night after supper the Bryans would gather around the piano to sing hymns as Mrs. Bryan played. Silas was a judge who had a deep faith in God. He never missed a chance to share the Gospel with others. He often prayed in court before making a decision. He shared the power of prayer with his family: "Willy, don't you ever forget when you get in a tough situation that the first thing to do is pray."[66]

Willy decided early in life that he wanted to be a lawyer. He loved to sit on the courthouse steps listening to the lawyers arguing their cases before his father. His mother was just as devoted to the Lord as her husband. She taught her children to always speak well of others. She homeschooled all of them. After lessons were over, the children delighted to run and play in the woods or hunt for squirrels or rabbits. Each day at lunchtime, Judge Bryan would read Willy a chapter from the Book of Proverbs. They would discuss it together. Then it was time for family prayer.

Life Decisions

In 1870, Judge Bryan told 10-year-old Willy and his sister, Fanny, that they would start attending classes in a one-room schoolhouse less than a mile away. Willy, now called Will, made friends easily. However, if the other boys used bad words, he would quietly walk away. He had learned from his mother this was wrong. When Will was 12 years old, his father ran for the U.S. Congress. Will was thrilled as he traveled about with his father, listening to the speeches and hearing people applaud. His father lost the race, but Will never lost his taste for politics.

Will was faithful to attend church and Sunday School every week. He and Fanny attended revival camp meetings. There, after a few nights of persuasive preaching, both Will and Fanny responded and placed their faith in Christ as their Lord and Savior.

Whipple Academy

Will attended Whipple Academy in Jacksonville, Illinois, to prepare him to enter Illinois College. The Academy was on the same campus as the college. The course of study included entering the oratory contest each year. This excited Will. The students were to choose a famous speech and practice oratory skills delivering it. Will's first entry was Patrick Henry's famous "Liberty or Death" speech. Will and a friend would go out on the nearby farm to practice speechmaking. Will worked hard but he was very nervous and failed to place at all.

Not discouraged, he determined to begin right away for next year's speech. He desperately wished to excel in oratory.

During his second year, he studied **Cicero**. He learned that Cicero had used persuasiveness in speeches when he defended righteousness. That sounded like what Will had learned from studying Proverbs. Following his father's example, he read and studied a chapter from the book of Proverbs each day. That year he came in third place in the oratory contest. The judge told him to work on pronouncing his words more clearly and not to speak so fast. Will determined to work on those problems. When practicing in the woods, he often tried talking with pebbles in his mouth. The Greek orator Demosthenes had done that to train himself to speak more clearly.

Cicero: A famous Roman statesman and orator

Illinois College

The following year Will enrolled in Illinois College. He was excited to be there. The professors were all Christians like his parents. He had heard of students who went away to other colleges and **forsook** their faith. The theory of evolution was creeping into higher education. This was the teaching that complex living beings, including people, just happened to develop from random changes in simpler life forms over millions of years; they

forsook: Abandoned

William Jennings Bryan — Champion of the Common Man

were not uniquely created by God. **Charles Darwin** was the principal author of this theory.

Will set out to confirm what he believed so he could explain it well to others. Some people believed in a combination of creation and evolution. Will studied hard and concluded that the Bible was true — that God created all living things in just six days. He told his friend who was entering the ministry, "I believe it (the Bible) will be just as valuable to me in the practice of law as it will be to you in the practice of the ministry."[67] That year, he won second place in an oratory contest. His hard work was paying off. He was beginning to get a reputation on campus as an orator. He began writing his own speeches, as well as memorizing those written by others. He determined to use oratory to work for justice for the ordinary working man.

> **Charles Darwin:** A British biologist responsible for thinking up the idea of evolution

Toward the end of his second year, he met a dark-haired girl with big brown eyes named Mary, a student at the nearby Jackson Female Academy. Mary loved Will's principled lifestyle and passion for truth. They began a friendship that eventually led to their marriage.

> **chaplain:** A mentor who provides spiritual care

Will enjoyed his last year in college. He became engaged to be married; he had the position of **chaplain** of his class; and he delivered the **valedictorian** address. He chose the topic of "character." Mary gave the valedictorian speech for her class as well. Then they parted ways until Will could get a job making enough money to support a family. Mary went home to her family to wait.

> **valedictorian:** The student with the highest grades chosen to speak to his class at graduation

Law School

Will moved to Chicago to attend Union College of Law. Here, he studied case law. He was required to read and study actual records of decisions made by judges, a method that trained students to think quickly and accurately. Will's favorite area of study was constitutional law. During his time at Union College, he continued to attend church faithfully and became involved in working with the **YMCA**. Students were discussing the big, life-changing issues of the day. These were the **prohibition of alcohol**,

> **YMCA:** Young Men's Christian Association

> **prohibition of alcohol:** Making it against the law to make or sell alcohol

William Jennings Bryan — Champion of the Common Man

women's right to vote, and whether to make other nations pay a **tariff** on items they purchase from the United States. Will was strongly in favor of prohibition and women's right to vote, but he was against tariffs. Will graduated from Union College of Law in June and received his master's degree. He then gave his attention to building up his law practice.

> **women's right to vote:** Women were not allowed to vote at this time
>
> **tariff:** Tax

Will and Mary were married on October 1, 1884. His law practice was growing and doing well. A year after their wedding, they had a baby daughter. Will set a schedule that he kept as long as they had children in the home. After breakfast, Will read to his family from the Bible, often using the Book of Proverbs the way his father did. Then, the family would sing hymns around the piano, followed by a time of prayer. Will taught Sunday school and was involved in programs to help the poor.

Politics

Will still had a strong desire to run for office. Mary reminded him that God would make a way for him at the right time. During the summer of 1887, he visited a friend from college who was living in Lincoln, Nebraska. Lincoln was a frontier town and Will was fascinated by it. It seemed to be growing quickly and had great possibilities for a lawyer.

Mary was willing to move so he set out to build a house for the family. He and his friend opened a law office together.

Most of Lincoln's growth was due to the railroad which carried settlers out west. Railroad monopolies owned some of the best property in the state and were a powerful force in the state government. They used this power to influence some state legislators to pass unfair laws that would benefit the railroads. Will decided if he ever ran for office, he would never be swayed by the railroad bosses.

Will moved his family to a lovely house he had built in Lincoln. They got involved in the community. Will taught Sunday school again; he joined organizations such as the Chamber of Commerce, Rotary Club, Modern Woodmen, YMCA, and many more. His goal was to run for office, so he wanted to meet as many people as possible. The population in Lincoln was very strongly Republican. Will was enthusiastically supported by the Democratic party. The Democrats asked him to speak at their meetings.

The railroads controlled the cost of sending agricultural products to markets. This drastically cut into farmers' profits. Bryan believed Lincoln needed someone to speak on behalf of the farmers, and he began to do that. One night after delivering a speech, he said to his wife exuberantly, "Mary, I had a strange experience. Last night I found that I had power over the audience. I could move them as I chose. I have more than usual power as a speaker."[68] Mary and Will knelt by their bed and asked God to help Will use this power of speaking wisely to benefit the common people.

State Convention

Bryan was soon elected to speak at the state convention. He spoke up for the farmers, the laborers — the ordinary American citizens. He encouraged legislators to fight against oppressive big businesses. This speech brought him statewide recognition. He received an invitation to the National Democratic Convention in St. Louis. Bryan was asked to run as the Democratic candidate for the House of Representatives. Bryan challenged regular, everyday people to join him in his stand against big business: "I shall go forth to the conflict as David went to meet the giant of the Philistines, not relying on my own strength, but trusting to the righteousness of my cause."[69]

Bryan briskly stepped out on the campaign trail. All his speeches centered around trusts, tariffs, and money. He spoke simply, so even children understood him. He told farmers, "When the poor and weak cry out for relief, they too often hear no answer while the rich, the strong, the powerful are given an attentive ear."[70] Everywhere he went, crowds flocked to hear him. He challenged his opponent to a debate and received thunderous applause from his audience. He won the debate, exciting the people with his views.

Congressman Bryan

Thirty-year-old William Jennings Bryan beat his opponent on election day by more than 6,000 votes. He became the second Democrat in the history of Nebraska to go to Congress. There he studied the money situation. He became convinced that if the government would use silver as well as gold for coins, more money would be available. That would help solve the financial crisis of the farmers.

He was appointed to the **Ways and Means Committee**. This was almost unheard of for a first-term congressman. When speakers addressed the topic of tariffs, audiences usually got bored, but not when Bryan spoke. The Senate **chamber** filled and overflowed with listeners when he spoke in support of a bill to reduce the tariff on imported wool. His speech was printed in newspapers — 100,000

Ways and Means Committee: The powerful Congressional committee tasked with making financial decisions for the government

chamber: The room in the U.S. Capitol where the Senate meets

copies were sold, and William Jennings Bryan became known across the nation as a powerful leader in Congress. Bryan was re-elected. He was nicknamed "The Gold-Tongued Orator."

Famous Speech

In his speech at the Democratic National Convention, Will sought to convince people to accept silver as **currency** rather than relying only on gold. His listeners were spellbound. He stood up for various groups of people — farmers, merchants, laborers, miners. Each group cheered as he mentioned them. The stirring conclusion echoed around the world as the battle cry of the silver movement. Delegates broke into cheering, waving handkerchiefs and hats. They pushed through the crowd to shake his hand. As a result of this speech, he became a candidate for president of the United States. At 36 years old, he was the youngest man ever to be nominated for president.

currency: Something that can be used to pay for goods or services

Secretary of State: The presidential cabinet officer responsible for foreign affairs

On election day, the Bryans voted and then headed home for their usual Bible study, hymns, and prayer time. Bryan lost the election, but it was close. He was still very popular with the people. He was the nominee for president again in 1900 and 1908. He was never elected president but had great opportunities to spread his message. He served as Woodrow Wilson's **Secretary of State**.

Scopes Monkey Trials

William Jennings Bryan was most famous for his role as the prosecuting attorney in the 1925 Scopes "Monkey" trial. Bryan was convinced that Charles Darwin's theory of evolution was completely wrong. He claimed that God didn't work through evolution but through miracles. He traveled to churches and schools speaking on the evils of evolution. He spoke before state legislatures to try to get them to prevent evolution from being taught in schools.

The state of Tennessee passed such a bill. However, a group of men from Tennessee didn't like the new law and decided to test it. John Scopes, a biology teacher in a local public school, had been teaching evolution. The **American Civil Liberties Union** agreed to pay legal fees for any teacher who was taken to court for violating the new law. They approached John Scopes. He showed them the book he had used: the official biology textbook approved by Tennessee which taught evolution.

The ACLU lawyers explained to John Scopes that they were looking for a case to try to **overturn** the new law; it wouldn't cost John anything. He reluctantly agreed. He

American Civil Liberties Union: A non-profit human rights organization that is supposed to defend individual freedoms

overturn: Throw out

William Jennings Bryan — Champion of the Common Man

didn't realize he had just consented to be part of one of the most famous trials of the century.

The ACLU chose a lawyer named Clarence Darrow. He was a brilliant debater, and he was an **atheist**. He also liked taking cases no one else wanted. When the trial began, every seat in the courtroom was full and people were standing outside. It was obvious that Scopes had broken the new law by teaching from the "approved" book. In his defense argument, Darrow said he would prove that the law actually had two parts to it. It said that evolution could not be taught, but also that Divine creation could not be denied. He argued that both parts of the law had to be broken to find Scopes guilty. He said Scopes had not denied the theory of Divine creation and therefore should not be found not guilty.

> **atheist:** A person who does not believe in God

William Jennings Bryan poured his heart and soul into standing for truth and defending biblical creation. He denounced Darrow's belief that man had descended from monkeys. At the end of eight days, John Scopes was found guilty of violating the new law and was fined $100.

This would be equivalent to almost $2,000 today. As a result of the trial, the issue of evolution had been discussed nationwide, and parents were made aware of what was being taught in the schools.

Bryan made arrangements to have his prepared speech printed and distributed. He believed this would answer the question of evolution once and for all. On the way home from the trial, he made several stops, giving speeches to over 50,000 people. Speaking of the trial he said, "It was a great victory for Christianity and a staggering blow to the forces of darkness."[71] He also met with a group of men who wanted to start the first **fundamentalist** university in America. It is named Bryan College after the famous orator.

> **fundamentalist:** Belief in the strict interpretation of Scripture

William Jennings Bryan — Champion of the Common Man

Just five days after the trial, Will told Mary he was going to take a short nap on the porch. Two hours later she found him dead. People made a great outpouring of love and displays of honor in his memory. The pastor who preached at his funeral told the crowd that he had come to Christ through the influence of one of Bryan's speeches. In a final prayer, another pastor prayed, "We thank Thee for this hero of the common people."[72] William Jennings Bryan achieved his life goal of using his talent for oratory to defend righteousness. He was truly a champion for the common man.

Glossary

affluent: Wealthy.

agony: Pain.

aide-de-camp: Confidential assistant.

Alamo: An old Catholic mission used as a fort.

allegiance: Commitment.

alma mater: The school from which one graduates.

altercation: An angry dispute.

amendments: Changes or additions.

American Civil Liberties Union: A non-profit human rights organization that is supposed to defend individual freedoms.

appeal: Make a serious request.

apprentice: Make one learn a trade from a skilled worker.

aptly: Skillfully.

architect: Designer.

arduous: Hard, difficult.

articulate: Able to express thoughts clearly.

assault: Attack.

asylum: Safe place.

atheist: A person who does not believe in God.

attributed: Gave credit to.

augment: Add to.

bifocal: Lenses for both close and distant vision.
board: Let them live in their homes.
boycott: Refuse to buy.
brethren: Those loved like family.
Cabinet: The presidential advisory body.
carried: Would be heard.
Chamber: The room in the U.S. Capitol where the Senate meets.
chaplain: A mentor who provides spiritual care.
Charles Darwin: A British biologist responsible for thinking up the idea of evolution.
Cicero: A famous Roman statesman and orator.
circulated: Passed around.
clerk: An administrative position.
cobblestones: Small round stones placed along the edges of streets.
commemorating: Remembering and honoring.
commissioned: Given the rank.
commodities: Economic goods.
common: Working class.
Commons: Park.
compelling: Convincing.
confiscate: Take possession of.
contemplated: Thought about.
contentious: Quarrelsome.
cover: Pay from his own money.
coyly: With cute or casual playfulness.

cross-examine: Ask questions of.

crowning glory: Greatest achievement.

currency: Something that can be used to pay for goods or services.

deacon: A servant leader in the church.

deference: Respect.

depression: Economic loss.

detrimental: Damaging.

dictated: Read aloud.

dispatch: Notice.

distinguished: Excellent.

distress: Troubles.

drought: Not enough rain.

duel: A combat with weapons fought between two persons in the presence of witnesses.

duty: Tax.

electrifying: Thrilling.

endeavor: Effort.

Ensign: Commissioned officer.

entreaty: A plea or petition.

epidemic: Widespread disease outbreak.

etched: Remembered clearly.

eulogy: Something written about one who died.

evangelist: Traveling preacher of the Gospel.

extensive: Large.

fervor: Passion.

flagship: A ship that carries the commanding admiral.

foresee: See beforehand.

forged: Beat into shape.

forsook: Abandoned.

fundamentalist: Belief in the strict interpretation of Scripture.

Governor Thomas Hutchinson: The British-appointed governor of the colony of Massachusetts.

grievances: Complaints.

Hessian: German.

horse litter: Bed pulled between two horses.

impenetrable: Hard to get to.

industry: Hard work.

inevitable: Unavoidable.

infallibility: Inability to be wrong.

infirmities: Illnesses.

input: Advice.

instigators: Persons behind a uprising.

intensified: Grew stronger.

interment: Burial.

investors: People who put money into something expecting to make a profit.

mentor: Teacher and advisor.

mercantile house: A business that shipped goods all over the world.

mercenaries: Soldiers hired for money.

merchant: A person who buys and sells goods.

45. David Collins, *Francis Scott Key: God's Courageous Composer* (Fenton, MI: Mott Media, 1982), 89.
46. Patterson, *Francis Scott Key: Poet and Patriot,* 61.
47. Collins, *Francis Scott Key: God's Courageous Composer* ,92.
48. Patterson, *Francis Scott Key: Poet and Patriot,* 63.
49. Ibid., 71.
50. Ibid., 79
51. Charles Lanman, *The Private Life of Daniel Webster* (Harper & Brothers, 1852), 100, 103.
52. Robert Allen, *Daniel Webster: Defender of the Union* (Milford, MI: Mott Media, 1989), 7.
53. Ibid., 64.
54. Ibid., 64.
55. Ibid., 81.
56. Ibid., 95.
57. Lanman, *The Private Life of Daniel Webster,* 100.
58. Jean Lee Latham, *Sam Houston: Hero of Texas* (New York: Chelsea House Publishers, 1961), 34.
59. William Johnson, *Sam Houston: The Tallest Texan* (New York: Random House, 1953), 21.
60. Latham, *Sam Houston: Hero of Texas,* 38.
61. Johnson, *Sam Houston: The Tallest Texan,* 48.
62. Ibid., 74.
63. Ibid., 78.
64. Latham, *Sam Houston: Hero of Texas,* 83.
65. Ibid., 70.
66. Robert A. Allen, *William Jennings Bryan: Golden-Tongued Orator* (Milford, MI: Mott Media, 1992), 6.
67. Ibid., 27.
68. Ibid., 55.
69. Ibid., 61.
70. Ibid., 62.
71. Ibid., 152.
72. Ibid., 154.

Endnotes

1. Elbridge S. Brooks, *The True Story of Benjamin Franklin: The American Statesman* (Boston, MA: Lothrop, Lee, and Shepherd Co., 1898), 19.
2. Ibid., 19.
3. Rick and Marilyn Boyer, *The Fight for Freedom* (Green Forest, AR: Master Books, 2015), 30.
4. Ibid., 35.
5. Henry Gilpin, ed., *The Papers of James Madison, Volume 2* (New York: J. & H.G. Langley, 1841), 984–986.
6. Brooks, *The True Story of Benjamin Franklin: The American Statesman*, 225.
7. Ibid., 227.
8. Charles A. Goodrich, *Lives of the Signers to the Declaration of Independence* (New York: Thomas Mather, 1837), 282.
9. Wilbur F. Gordy, *American Leaders and Heroes* (New York: Charles Scribner and Sons, 1904), 158.
10. Ibid., 160.
11. William H. Mace, *Mace's School History of the United States* (Chicago, IL: Rand McNally & Company, 1904), 156.
12. Ann Heinrichs, *Samuel Adams: Father of the Revolution* (Chanhassen, MN: The Child's World, 2004), 23.
13. Benjamin H. Irvin, *Samuel Adams: Son of Liberty, Father of the Revolution* (New York: Oxford University Press, 2002), 159.
14. Ibid., 165.
15. Nardi Reeder Campion, *Patrick Henry: Firebrand of the Revolution* (Boston, MA: Little, Brown, and Company, 1961), 50.
16. Ibid., 60.
17. Ibid., 85.
18. Ibid., 85.
19. Ibid., 85.
20. Ibid., 94.
21. Ibid., 97.
22. Wilbur F. Gordy, *American Leaders and Heroes* (New York: Charles Scribner's Sons, 1904), 154.
23. Ibid., 154.
24. Ibid., 154.
25. Ibid., 154.
26. Campion, *Patrick Henry: Firebrand of the Revolution,* 179.
27. Charles River Editors, *American Legend: The Life of John Hancock* (Ann Arbor, MI: CreateSpace Independent Publishing Platform, 2013), 9.
28. Ibid., 17.
29. Ibid., 34.
30. Jean Fritz, *Alexander Hamilton: The Outsider* (New York: Puffin Books, 2011), 52.
31. Pam Pollack, *Who Was Alexander Hamilton?* (New York: Penguin Random House, 2017), 100–101.
32. Ibid., 101.
33. Helen Stone Peterson, *Henry Clay: Leader in Congress* (New York: Chelsea House Publishers, 1991), 45.
34. Ibid., 48.
35. Ibid., 58.
36. Ibid., 61.
37. Ibid., 64.
38. Ibid., 77.
39. Ibid., 77–78.
40. Ibid., 80.
41. Lillie Patterson, *Francis Scott Key: Poet and Patriot* (Philadelphia, PA: Chelsea House Publishers, 1991), 22.
42. Ibid., 24.
43. Ibid., 42.
44. Ibid., 42.

Chapter 5

America's Story Vol. 1
Children's Atlas of the U.S.A.
The Fight for Freedom

America's Struggle to Become a Nation
Passport to America
Language Lessons for a Living Education

Chapter 6

America's Story Vol. 1
Children's Atlas of the U.S.A.
The Fight for Freedom

America's Struggle to Become a Nation
Passport to America
Language Lessons for a Living Education

Chapter 7

America's Story Vol. 1
Children's Atlas of the U.S.A.
The Fight for Freedom

America's Struggle to Become a Nation
Passport to America
Language Lessons for a Living Education

Chapter 8

America's Story Vol. 1
Children's Atlas of the U.S.A.
The Fight for Freedom

America's Struggle to Become a Nation
Passport to America
Language Lessons for a Living Education

Chapter 9

America's Story Vol. 1
Children's Atlas of the U.S.A.
The Fight for Freedom

America's Struggle to Become a Nation
Passport to America
Language Lessons for a Living Educatio

Chapter 10

America's Story Vol. 2
Children's Atlas of the U.S.A.

Passport to America
Language Lessons for a Living Education

Corresponding Curriculum

The *What a Character! Series* can be used alongside other Master Books curriculum for reading practice or to dive deeper into topics that are of special interest to students.

This book in the series features famous American statesmen, whose stories would incorporate well for students in grades 6–8 accompanying history, language arts, vocabulary words and definitions, as well as geography studies and cultural insights. We have provided the list below to help match this book with related Master Books curriculum.

Chapter 1

America's Story Vol. 1 — *America's Struggle to Become a Nation*
Children's Atlas of the U.S.A. — *Passport to America*
The Fight for Freedom — *Language Lessons for a Living Education*

Chapter 2

America's Story Vol. 1 — *America's Struggle to Become a Nation*
Children's Atlas of the U.S.A. — *Passport to America*
The Fight for Freedom — *Language Lessons for a Living Education*

Chapter 3

America's Story Vol. 1 — *America's Struggle to Become a Nation*
Children's Atlas of the U.S.A. — *Passport to America*
The Fight for Freedom — *Language Lessons for a Living Education*

Chapter 4

America's Story Vol. 1 — *America's Struggle to Become a Nation*
Children's Atlas of the U.S.A. — *Passport to America*
The Fight for Freedom — *Language Lessons for a Living Education*

What a Character! READERS FOR KIDS
Notable Lives from History

Inspire Students with Biographies of Notable Lives from HISTORY.

MASTERBOOKS.COM — *Where Faith Grows!*

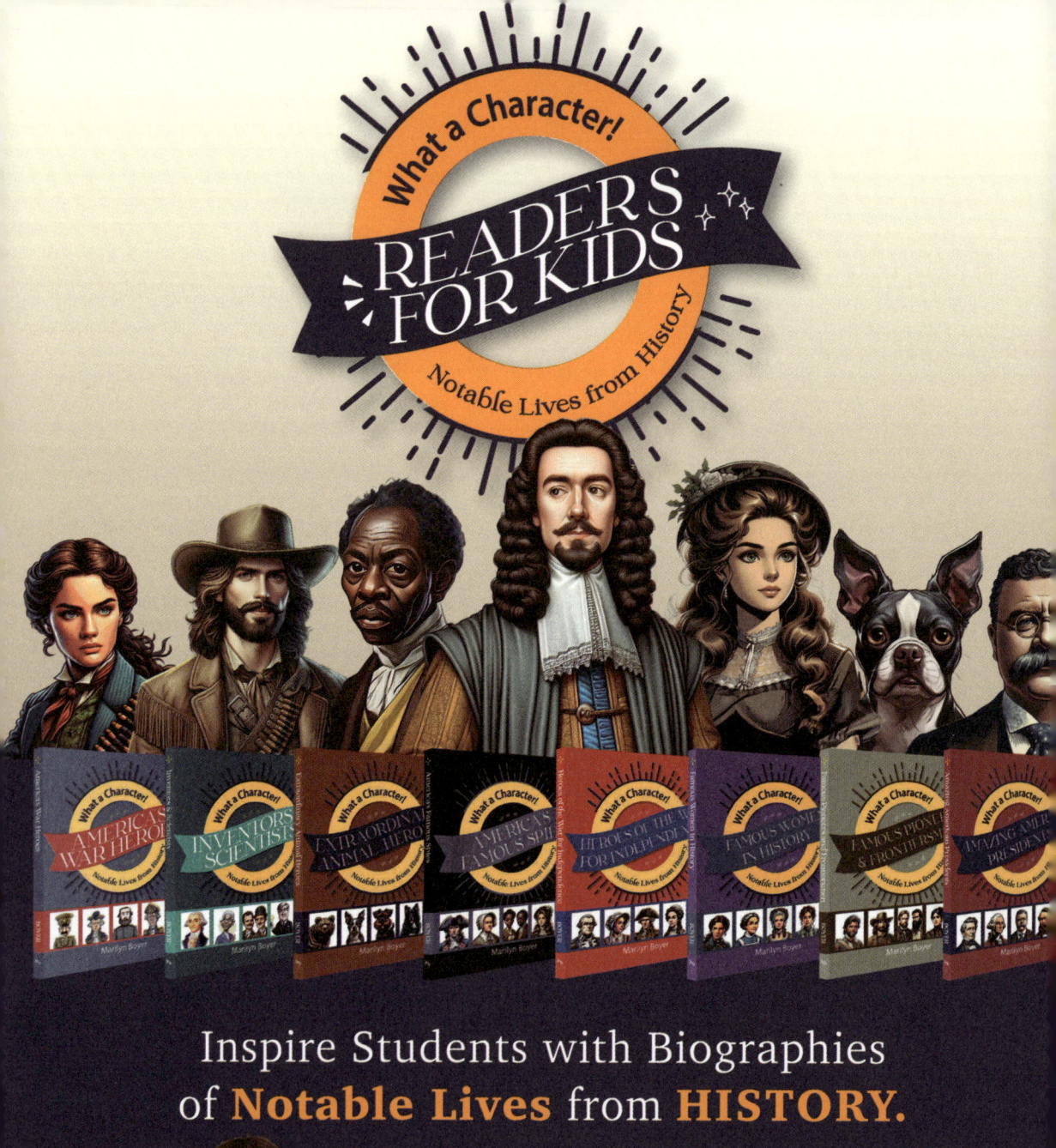

America's War Heroes
Inventors and Scientists
Extraordinary Animal Heroes
Heroes of the War of Independence

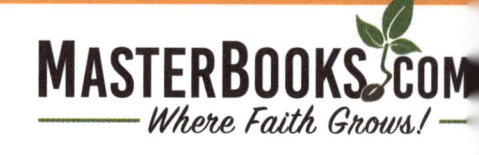

Famous Women in History
Famous Pioneers and Frontiersm[en]
Amazing American Presidents
America's Famous Spies